GRACE OVER THE LONG RUN

AN AUTOBIOGRAPHY OF A MISSIONARY AND PASTOR WHO IS NOT PERFECT

GEORGE PONTIUS

iUniverse, Inc.
Bloomington

GRACE OVER THE LONG RUN
An autobiography of a missionary
and pastor who is not perfect

iUniverse books may be ordered through booksellers or by contacting:

iUniverse
1663 Liberty Drive
Bloomington, IN 47403
www.iuniverse.com
1-800-Authors (1-800-288-4677)

*Because of the dynamic nature of the Internet, any Web addresses or links
contained in this book may have changed since publication and may no longer
be valid.*

ISBN: 978-1-4502-6448-8 (sc)
ISBN: 978-1-4502-6453-2 (ebk)

Printed in the United States of America

iUniverse rev. date: 12/06/2010

ACKNOWLEDGMENT

For years as I have shared stories of my life experiences from childhood throughout my years in the Navy, College, Marriage, Missionary and Pastor. I have been asked to put them in writing. More than once I have started only to stop because the desire would fade. However, recently the urging of members of my former congregation and friends has led me to set down my story of joy, sorrow, failures, salvation, and victory as it demonstrates God's grace over the long run.

I am not famous. I hold no lofty position. Great men write books. Famous men of God are sought after by publishing houses. I am none of these. My story is simply a true one of the lesser of God's servants and his experience of God's grace through difficult times to find the Lord Jesus faithful as He promised. Deuteronomy 31:6 promises grace over the long run.

> "Be strong and courageous. Do not be
> afraid or terrified because of them for the

> LORD your God goes with you. He will
> never leave you nor forsake you." (NIV)

To whom shall I dedicate this book? Naturally, first to my Lord and Savior, Jesus Christ, Who has been there through joy and sorrow, failure and victory. He has shown over and over that His mercy and grace endure forever. Secondly, I dedicate this book to my dear wife of fifty three years, Marilyn. She has stood by me literally in sickness and in sorrow, in plenty and in want, in failure and in victory. Without her I would not be sitting here telling my life's story. And also I dedicate this book to my children who found that their father was less than perfect, to say the least, yet loved him still. Thirdly, this book is dedicated to Pastor Edward Underhill and Dr. "Nick" Faber. Under their personal friendship that spans forty years, spiritual guidance and their holding me accountable to the Word of God, I have been loved, accepted and encouraged to get up and go on and to minister the Word in the grace that I myself have received. Lastly, the Body of Believers who have loved and encouraged, and stood behind me over the past fifty years, and to all of God's servants who find that they are not perfect, but still human, struggle with the past, with depression, with failures and even breakdowns. There is hope in the midst of despair…joy in the midst of sorrow…strength when none can be found in yourself.

I owe much to our sons and their families who have often shown me the way through the wilderness by their own examples of living grace. God bless you all.

George Pontius

CONTENTS

ACKNOWLEDGMENT v

FOREWARD xi

INTRODUCTION xiii

PART I 1

CHAPTER ONE - a Slide Show of Memories 3
    BUSTER. 4
    LIGHT AND SHADOWS. 5
    CHRIST FOR ME. 10
    THE DUNGEON 12

CHAPTER TWO - Human Angels 17
    AN ANGEL OF MUSIC 17
    PRINCIPALS CAN BE ANGELS TOO 19

CHAPTER THREE - Semper Fi 26
    TAKING ORDERS 26
    THE GOOK CEMETERY. 30
    OF SILENT BATTLEFIELD. 32
    RECKLESS. 34

CHAPTER FOUR - Preparation
    for the Lord's Service 41
    HOME AT LAST. 41
    THE CATTLE DRIVE 43

EXPERIMENT IN BLACK AND WHITE.... 54

THAT'S MORE LIKE IT 59

NEWLY WEDS 61

THE PRISON 65

SURFING TO MINISTRY 71

IN MEMORY OF GABRELLA RAMOS...... 77

CHAPTER FIVE - "Honey, We're Home" 80

GOOD BYE............................ 80

"HONEY, WE'RE HOME"............... 83

THE COMPOUND 85

KARUIZAWA........................... 89

CLIMB THE MOUNTAIN............... 96

PLEASE NOT NOW, LORD.............. 98

CHAPTER SIX - The Mountains Shall Sing...... 103

THE DOG............................ 103

CRUSADES AND PRISON MINISTRY..... 106

CHAPLAINS AND DOLLS 109

THE TELEGRAM 113

I HATE GOD 115

THE FRUIT OF THE WORD 119

CHAPTER SEVEN - Reunion and Reports 121

HOMEWARD BOUND 121

FURLOUGHS ARE NOT REST.......... 126

CHAPTER EIGHT - Return to Japan 130

VISITORS FROM HOME 131

FOUR MONTHS THIS TIME............ 135

PART II **141**

CHAPTER NINE - The Dream Ends........... 143

GOD'S PLANS, NOT OURS 143

OUR WEST SIDE STORY 144

CHAPTER TEN - Millions of Yen 148
   BOXES OF MONEY 148
   RIVERVIEW 152

CHAPTER ELEVEN - A Matter of Repentance . . . 155
   DEALING WITH FAILURE 157
   SURVIVING THE STORM 158

CHAPTER TWELVE - Climbing Up Again 160
   IN CHRIST EVERYONE IS SOMEONE 160
   BACK PACKING AND SUCH 161
   PROBLEMS, PARENTS AND PASTORS 163

CHAPTER THIRTEEN - Dare We Try Again? . . . 166
   GOD'S SUPPLY 166
   A KNOCK AT THE DOOR 168
   A Backpack Never Forgotten 169
   CONFRONTED BY DEMONS 173
   DETERMINED TO DIE 177

CHAPTER FOURTEEN - Minirth Meier
      Psychiatric Hospital 179
   APPLYING GRACE AND TRUTH OVER
      TIME 179
   IN THE PULPIT AGAIN 184
   TESTED BY DEATH 187
   RUSSIA 190
   ISRAEL 198
   COPENHAGEN 205

EPILOGUE - Wrapping Up the Theme 207
   Grace Over the Long Run 207

FOREWARD

Dr. Martin Nick Faber

I was alone at home when George and Marilyn stopped by to leave a copy of this book with me. After we had discussed the book George asked if I would like to go for something to eat. One does not ask a full-blooded Dutchman if he would like to eat so off we went. We visited for two hours. Marilyn mentioned that the evening was like "old times", except Beverly, my wife, was missing. Part of our time was used attempting to identify when we first met. We decided it was the mid-nineteen forties when George came to Whitworth College (now University) to visit his brother, Lester. Lester and I lived in the same dormitory at the time.

Our children had a "BLAST" while our families grew up together. George and Marilyn provided the boys and Beverly and I the girls. Beverly and I have five children, the four eldest being girls and George and Marilyn have four boys. We enjoyed watching this next generation develop deep friendships as well.

One of my favorite memories of Marilyn took place at our "rustic" cabin on beautiful Palmer Lake in North Central Washington. Beverly and I had encouraged George and Marilyn to spend time at the cabin while they were back in Spokane for a few weeks from missionary work. Our family supported them through prayer, finances and friendship in this endeavor. We were pleased when they accepted our suggestion. Later, when we used the cabin there on the wall was a striking painting of the lake and mountains. Marilyn, a gifted artist, must have spent hours completing that painting. It now is a valued and treasured part of our cabin and reminds us of our long-standing and mutual friendship and respect.

Another great moment with the Pontius' was at our home. Three young Japanese students attending Whitworth came to our house for dinner. The girls were impressed and delighted to be greeted and converse with George and Mariln in their native language. They made three young ladies feel at home and welcomed in a way few could have. Their warmth and charm made the evening a special delight for all.

Beverly and I have felt honored to have the Pontius family be our close and trusted friends. They have been friends through good times and difficult times. Their trust in God never seemed to waver even through extremely stressful times. The constant peace and joy they showed was encouraging to me. These trials were an opportunity for Beverly and I to minister to them as they lived through them. It was a privilege to be able to do this.

Our family appreciates being valued by George and Marilyn and family and that we continue to be friends. George, thank you for taking the time and energy to complete this book. May God have the glory and honor!

INTRODUCTION

Over the years of ministry I have read many stories of great Christians. The conclusion to which I came is that I will never be like them because there is too much of my old nature with which I still struggle. My heart was fixed on God, but my daily experience was influenced by the old nature. I began to wonder if these people about whom I read and pastors I knew personally were some kind of angelic creatures. Never once was a human error mentioned. Their pedestals were of polished granite. To suggest that they got mad, or had other "hangovers" from their old nature was unthinkable. In fact, I met a missionary one time who was being dismissed from her field because she had written a newsletter telling of her spiritual struggles. "Missionaries don't have spiritual struggles," she was told. "If they do, it is never to be made known to their supporters. After all they are to be the height of spirituality." She was devastated. Instead of receiving understanding counsel she was dismissed. My own experience belies the teaching that missionaries are super-spiritual.

So I labored with this book. Reading the Psalms one day I realized that God told the truth about David yet called him "a man after My own heart" (Acts 13:22 NIV) I think David was given that title not because he was perfect, but because he did not hide his weaknesses and sin for long. We get a peek into the heart of David from Psalm 27:3 "When Thou saidest, seek ye my face, my heart said unto Thee, Thy face, O LORD, will I seek." (KJV) David had a truly humble heart.

So my story from the beginning is like a slide show. There are some beautiful, colorful slides in the program, but in between there are dark pictures. The darkness is fleeting sometimes and lingers at others. There are periods of my life when the darkness overwhelms the light. By the grace of God the darkness could not extinguish the light. My story is one of God's unconditional love and grace - GRACE OVER THE LONG RUN.

It is my hope that you will concentrate on the eternal grace of God over the long run in your life. God's unconditional grace is eternal and does not dim even in the darkness. It shines with His light and over the long run it triumphs over all darkness no matter how thick. When we have learned to "walk in the light as He is in the light, the blood of Jesus Christ, God's Son, continues to cleanse us from all sin and we have fellowship with Him and with each other". (1 John 1:9 - my paraphrase)

May God bless you as you read.

George Pontius

PART I

CHAPTER ONE

A SLIDE SHOW OF MEMORIES

BUSTER

My earliest memories are of the farm in Mabton, Washington. My grandfather Hiram Kauffman had homesteaded that farm in 1911. My parents were running the farm after my Grandmother's death and my Grandfather's failing health. These memories are filled with the farm animals I loved. Best of all was my dog, Mike. I had three lambs, Blackie, Whitey, and Ewey. We had a big work-horse, Buster, that I liked to ride by the time I was two years old. My older brother, Lester, and my cousin, Tom, would often lift me up between them on Buster and off we'd go bareback. There were also cats, rabbits, pigs, and cows. And of course everywhere were chickens of all sizes.

Then there was Grandpa, my very best friend in the world. I felt safe with him. Here's where the first dark slide comes into view. My mother was often ill from the time I was born. Grandpa thus became my constant companion. I have very few memories of my mother in those days She did keep a baby book from which I get a glimpse of her. Two statements from that book shed light on those days. She writes: "One of his expressions which touches mother's heart is "Put yous arms around me mama, I's scared." At a later date I got to go shopping with my mother in the old touring car. She writes, "June 6, 1936" (I was three), "I was going to leave George in the car while I did some shopping and this was his argument to go along, "You better not leave me mama, 'cause I had a little boy, and I left him the car, and the car started to go backwards and the little boy was killed." I have often pondered where a three year old would come up with such a thought.

Not long after that we moved to Spokane, Washington. The memories of mother are still very dim. One night I was awakened by a terrifying scene. People were yelling and sirens were screaming. I could see a red glow in the back of the house. My Dad grabbed me and ran into the front yard. Everyone was there including Grandpa. I could see the flames shooting out of the back porch. Then I realized that my dog, Laddie, was not there Grandpa said he was still in the basement. To my relieve a fireman came out of the basement with Laddie in his arms. In my memory I can see the eerie scene with furniture hauled to the front yard and covered with canvas. Even the smell of the smoke remains. Yet, nowhere in my memory do I remember seeing my mother, though I know she was there. We lived in what was left of that house for a few weeks until we could move to the home from which most of my mid-childhood memories come. There I made some new friends, began school and we all joined Fourth Presbyterian Church. I adjusted well to the loss of my farm animal friends. We would never return to the farm.

LIGHT AND SHADOWS

Grandpa had great stories to tell. I would crawl onto his lap and he would light his pipe - I loved the smell of that pipe - and begin a story. "Well, sir", he'd say and I knew I was in for a great story. Many were about the Ol' West or the Civil War where his brothers fought, one of them,

Lemmel, giving his life in that conflict. Grandpa was about ten years old when President Abraham Lincoln was shot. Then there were tales of his riding "shotgun" on a stagecoach. He was my *real* cowboy hero. We both listened to the famous radio show "Tom Mix" faithfully every day. It was just Grandpa and me. I hadn't yet entered school. Every afternoon I would sit on his lap while he read to me the comics, or one of my favorite books. "Oh, do I have to read *Clarabelle The Cow* again?" But, before I could answer his voice took on a magical tone as he'd begin, "Well sir…" while lighting his pipe.

I had some new friends. One, Donny, was from two houses away, and a couple from church. One of my best friends was Dick, our pastor's son. There wasn't anything that we didn't get into. We were both always on the go never stopping for a moment. One early morning after we had camped out in his back yard we woke up about 5 a.m. and ran screaming like Indians around the house. Shortly, his father, my pastor, came out the door with a paddle in his hand and gave us a good spanking. It was Saturday and his day to sleep in.

Later in I found out that I was ADHD (Attention Deficit Hyperactive Disorder) which was at the root of my behavior. I also discovered in my late fifties that I still suffered from that disorder. In my childhood days noone understood the causes and I was labeled an "uncontrollable" boy. Teachers would pass on that report to the next teacher and I was "doomed" before the year began.

During grade school one of my best friends was Jerry with whom I still have contact. Another good friend was Evan whom I still see occasionally. His father was our local druggist. Evan had a bicycle. Because we could not afford things like that I envied him and his bike. Evan was a great friend and often lent me his bike. One day I rode to the gas station nearby and decided to put more air in the tires. Of course I had no idea what I was doing. The result was a blown tire. I was terrified that I would get in trouble. However, I pushed the bicycle home thinking what Evan's dad would do. To my delight both Evan and his dad were very calm and understanding. They were just glad that I was not hurt. I learned that day what it meant to be a true friend.

Every Sunday we went to church. I had to sit with my parents in adult church. Of course the Pastor's message was beyond my understanding. My parents gave me a piece of paper and I would draw the picture that was in one of the stained glass windows of the church. It was of Jesus knocking at a door. The window is still there with all its memories. It played a significant part in my decision to open my heart's door. I guess I was rowdy in Sunday School. Later, when as an adult and was Associate Pastor of that church, a former Sunday School teacher in my first and second grades confided to me, somewhat sheepishly, that I was the only child she prayed for on Saturday night whom she ask God that I would not show up in the morning. We laughed a lot about that. But even as an adult and a pastor the old pain from my childhood would grip deep inside me. And I really did not understand why such an innocent statement, said obviously out of respect and love for me, would be so hurtful. After all, I was a grown man and a pastor.

What was that verse we learned in Bible School as I was preparing for the ministry? Oh yes, *"Therefore, if any man be in Christ he is a new creature,* old *things are passed away, behold all things are become new."* (2 Corinthians 5:17 NIV). However, for me some of the "old things" just would not pass away.

Sometimes I get together with my grade school friend, Jerry. We share memories as we go over our school memories. We were in the same class. I seemed to attract bullies as well. One day I had just arrived at school for Mrs. "O"'s class. It was just before Christmas and we had a special project to make gifts for our mothers. I had brought a slender, green olive jar for the project. It had been no easy task to find one as we never had olives. But my grandpa had succeeded in getting one for me. I was very excited about this neat gift for momma that I was going to make. Outside on the playground some older boys saw me with the jar.

"What 'cha got in your pocket, sissy, Sunday School boy?", they sneered as they crowded me into the corner of the building.

"Noth…nothing", I hesitantly replied.

"Well, then, if it's nothing give it to us.," they demanded.

They grabbed the jar and before I could protest smashed it against the brick wall of the school. I was devastated. It was the last day we could bring our jars and the day we were going to work on them. The teacher would be mad at me, I thought. She would think that I was not listening again or just forgot. The boys had warned me about not telling. Worst of all there would be no Christmas gift for my mother. I waited until the very last ring of the bell before I entered the school. Mrs. "O" was at the class room door. She stooped down so she could see my face, now muddied with dirt and tears, the pieces of the broken bottle in my hands. She didn't ask me who did it, but only if someone had broken my jar. I was so glad she hadn't asked me who. Standing up she took my small hand and led me to her desk. She said that God has a way of working out bad things. And with that she opened the bottom drawer of her desk revealing several olive jars. Reaching in she took one and put it in my hand and with her finger wiped the tears from my eyes "Now", she said, "your mother will have a great present from you." She was my "angel" from then on. The worst day became the happiest day. We cut up pieces of colored paper and glued them randomly on the jar in our own pattern. Then we wrapped them ourselves in Christmas paper. I have never forgotten her kind deed to a little boy.

Mother was often absent in those days. Her health was failing and she often spent weeks in the hospital or nursing home. Dad had saved enough money to put down on a house of our very own. They had even picked out the house. I loved it with it's big front porch, grass in the yard, and my very own room. After church one Sunday we met with the realtor and Dad told him we would take the house. Mother had a doctor's appointment Monday morning and right after Dad would go to the bank and get the money for the down payment and bring it to the owner.

I couldn't wait for Mom and Dad to return from the doctor's office and the bank so we could go and buy the house. But it was not to be. Their faces looked frightened and both had tears in their eyes. Their life's dream had just been flushed down the toilet. Mother had breast cancer. The money was needed for radical surgery to save her life. She never fully recovered from the emotional blow that was to her.

CHRIST FOR ME

Growing up in a devoutly Christian home I learned the Bible from my mother's knee. "God is love" was the first Bible verse I memorized. Church was the highlight of the week for all of us. Sunday School was fun and I loved the crafts. I assumed I was a Christian since I had been baptized as a baby the same day my brother, Lester, was baptized. He is nine years older than I. But until I grew to the ripe age of eight or nine I never considered that I needed a personal relationship with Jesus Christ. In 1942 Christian Endeavor, a non-denominational youth organization, held it's annual convention at Westminister Congregational Church in downtown Spokane. For the first time I was able to attend such a big event. What an experience that was! I had been introduced to flannelgraph Bible stories through released time education at my school. However, I had never seen such beautiful pictures before. This is a method of telling a story while putting pictures on a background of flannel on an easel. Theme of the convention was *Christ For Me* and the theme song was entitled the same. We sang it several times a day during the conference that I decided that Christ was for me and I became a born-again Christian.

I was exceedingly happy and I did not want the convention to end. But it was only for a weekend and it was the last day, Saturday. Mom and Dad were coming to pick me up and take me with them to Lewiston, Idaho to visit my uncle and his family. So I had to leave that afternoon early and go to the busy corner to await them. I was totally oblivious to the busy street corner and the cars waiting for the light to change. The little chorus, *Christ For Me,* kept ringing in my ears and I started to sing it at the top of my voice. It ended with a strong high note. It was then I noticed the stopped cars, the people staring and the many smiles. Then I saw Mom and Dad in our car stopping by the curb-side. The windows were rolled down and Mom had tears in her eyes. At first I was greatly embarrassed as I realized everybody had been listening. Quickly I jumped into the back seat. I was so thankful that the light changed and we were off for our trip.

The wheat fields were golden to the harvest and the slight wind made waves through the stalks of grain as if crashing on a golden shore. My mouth was going like a freight train as I told Mom and Dad all about the convention and especially about my making a decision to believe in Jesus as my own Savior. Indeed it was *Christ For Me.*

It was about one hundred miles to Lewiston which included a long twisting drive down the Lewiston grade to the valley. There were no trees so one could see for miles. Many years later I was to learn that my future mother-in-law had traveled down that steep road, which was only dirt then, in a covered wagon sitting next to the driver holding her new-born little brother.

It was a beautiful sight. My mother, however, was terrified of height and Dad made her lie down so she did not have to see anything until we reached the Snake river. Soon I was awash in cousins. Running and playing together was an added prize. It was a wonderful weekend that I did not want to end. Nothing could ruin life now that I had Jesus in my life. I was wrong.

THE DUNGEON

The summer of 1940 was good. The Pontius Family Reunion was hosted by my parents and was held in Spokane. I eagerly looked forward to seeing all my aunts, uncles and cousins. There were dozens of them. What fun we had! The big Family Picnic was held in Mission Park. Just as we were getting ready to eat, lightening struck, thunder rolled and the rain poured. It was fun to watch the women grab the food and run for shelter while the men grabbed benches and put them under the gazebo. Unknown to us it would be several years before another one. America was at war. That summer I missed my brother who worked in the forest and was away from home. I missed his taking me to the pool and especially his making mud villages for my toy cars.

A couple of years before new neighbors had moved in next door. They had two teenage boys who were mean to me. They always threatened me that if I told on them something bad would happen to my family and I would be put in a dungeon and the door locked. They were much bigger than I so I told no one.

In the fall of 1942 my brother went to war. The house seemed empty without him. But Grandpa was there and that made things just right. By now my mother's cancer recovery was complete. In fact she seemed to be in the best health she had been in for a long time. My memories of her are clearer from the earlier days of WWII. I remember going on picnics. One day my brother caught an enormous frog at the river and brought it to our picnic spot. Mom was almost hysterical until Dad made Lester take it back to the river. There was a trip to the Barnum and Bailey Circus with Grandpa. And, of course many delightful times with my cousin, Gordon, who lived in Spokane and was closer to my age.

I remember that after the boys next door moved, I took stones and broke out all the windows in their house. It gave me great satisfaction to vent my anger at something other than myself. Of course my parents had to pay for the damages. Strangely, I do not recall their punishing me for that. Perhaps they knew somehow that something bad went on there.

`Christmas of 1942 came and went. Lester was in the Army. Dad and Mom had been buying candy bars for weeks from vending machines at Sears to include in the Christmas package they put together to send to Lester. My tenth birthday in 1943 my cousin Gordon and my friends, Donny and Evan celebrated with me along with Mom, Dad and Grandpa. I had written to a radio show for some florescent strips to put on the stairs and the doorposts that would glow during an air raid blackout drill. My father was an air raid warden and took his responsibility seriously. The nation was at war. There were bomb drills at school, scrap metal drives for the war effort and ration coupons for everything from gas, to shoes and food. As a ten year old it was very exciting. Of course the terror of war never crossed my young mind. Everything seemed to be going well until Valentines Day, 1943.

It was Sunday around two in the morning. Mom had been feeling very well when I went to bed. Two weeks earlier we had gone to visit friends after church. Mom had fallen and bruised her leg badly. The swelling had gone down and the pain in Mom's leg had subsided. The doctor with the best of intentions told Mother to exercise that leg and get the circulation going to reduce the swelling. He did not realize that a blood clot had formed in her leg and traveled with the blood to her lungs and brain. I woke up early on Valentines morning to the screams of my mother. She had the most excruciating headache she had ever experienced. She could not hold back her cries. Dad was on the phone calling the doctor. He could not come right away because he was out delivering a baby. No ambulance could be ordered until he came and examined Mom and authorized it himself.

In the meantime my father, who was beside himself with worry, put me in the side bedroom next to the neighbor's house, closed the door and locked it. It was like the dungeon the boys had warned me about. Was my mother dying? I thought it must be my fault, but I had not told on them. I could still hear the commotion outside my "dungeon" door. Grandpa and Dad were talking in muffled voices I was really scared. Then I heard the doctor come and soon after that the sirens of the ambulance were shrieking in the distance.

Finally, Dad opened the bedroom door and brought me out. My friend Donny's mother was there. She got me dressed and put me in a warm coat. I was to go with her to stay for the night. The stretcher with my mother on it was moved out the door and into the ambulance. As we went to Donny's house I glanced down the street to see the flashing red lights and hear the screaming sirens disappearing in the distance on their way to the hospital Then there was just the darkness of the night I would never see my mother alive again.

Dad returned from the hospital about noon and I came home. The phone rang. It was St. Luke's Hospital. Mom had died just twelve hours after I last seen her go out the door to the ambulance. She had suffered a cerebral hemorrhage caused by the traveling blood clot. The embolism was fatal. We arrived at the hospital about an hour later. Pastor was with us. She lay still upon the bed with a sheet covering her face. The nurse folded it back and I looked upon the first dead person I had ever been allowed to see. Rushing from the room, I ran crying down the hallway, not even knowing where I was going. Dad remained at Mom's side, disabled by grief. She was only fifty five years old. St. Luke's was run by the Episcopal Church. A kindly nun had seen me run down the hall and followed, She caught up with me as I entered a glassed-in solarium. I was screaming that it was all my fault. I felt her strong arms on my shoulder, turning me around. Instinctively I buried my head on her breast. She explained that God does not punish anyone by taking a loved one. She did not know why my mother had to die, but she knew God. He is loving and kind and loves me very much. I felt her tears drop on my head and I relaxed in her arms letting my tears flow softly. Shortly my Dad came for me. We held each other quietly. We notified the family of Mom's death. Our pastor was quick to comfort us. He and Dad made all the arrangements with the funeral home and cemetery. Then we left Mom behind and went home. I wanted to run immediately to Grandpa's arms, but my Uncle had taken him home with them. When Dad put the key in the door it was as silent as a tomb. Dad immediately started the long process of finding Lester and notifying him of Mother's death. Dad and I just sat down in silence. I soon fell asleep out of pure exhaustion. The next day at the funeral home we entered a very slow elevator that took us to the slumber room where I saw Mom again. I believe Lester had arrived and was with us. He took Mother's death rather hard. I avoided going into the "dungeon" as it was too frightening for me. I have no memory of Mom's funeral service or burial.

Weeks went by. Then one day Dad announced he was going to Seattle to see about a job his brother, my uncle had offered him. I stayed with friends while he was gone. Dad purchased a house in West Seattle which my uncle financed. We moved in early April.

My nightmares began with a dream. I was standing at the foot of a hill with Dad. While he remained I climbed the hill. On the other side was Mom standing beside her casket. I ran back down the hill to Dad. "Mom is not dead, she is alive, I joyously yelled. Taking Dad by the hand I led him up the hill and down the other side. However, when we got there Mom was lying dead in the casket. This dream continued well into adulthood.

As we boarded the train for Seattle I was both excited and sad. We had little money so I had to leave behind all my toys and precious things. I also missed my school, friends, relatives, and especially my Grandfather who was my special buddy. He had gone to live with my uncle. The train slowly moved out of town and across the trestle by the cemetery. I looked out of the window upon the graves below. Tears welled up as I quietly cried -

"Goodbye Mamma"

CHAPTER TWO

HUMAN ANGELS

AN ANGEL OF MUSIC

Moving to Seattle was a new beginning for me. I looked forward to seeing Puget Sound. There were new friends, new sights, new people, new sounds. But also new problems arose. Sometimes a child's hope is that everything would change all at once, and that with the change there would be no vestige of the old. But one learns quickly that life is not like that. The old influences the new. Today we have coined the tern "old baggage". Dad and I had hidden among our real luggage a lot of "old baggage". Dad was devastated by Mom's death. He began to slip into a long depression that nothing seemed to penetrate. He worked hard at my uncle's fuel yard. His hours at home were spent mostly in silence and sleep. He no longer cared about birthday parties or decorating for Christmas. These only caused him too much pain with Mother gone.

For me the first change was a new school. Since I had begun school in the mid-year, I was now in grade 5B. But with Mom's death and the turmoil surrounding it I had not kept with my studies. We moved in April, and my former school in Spokane somehow did not send my transcript to my new school in West Seattle. This caused my being put on "probation". I really didn't realize that this was simply an administrative procedure. I thought that I had failed once again. But God's Grace was there for the long run. He had plans for me and people to guide me in His plan of whom I had never dreamed. I remember these individuals as bright angelic stars on the horizon of my future.

I had begun violin lessons when I was five years old. I don't remember where I got the violin that was small and fit my chin. It was a gift from someone. I liked music and had often gone by myself to downtown Spokane for my lesson. Here in Seattle, at Gatewood Elementary school, there was a traveling music teacher who came three times a week. I was eager to sign up for violin lessons. They were group lessons, but that was all right with me. The first day we were given cards to fill out with our names, addresses etc. I did the best I could. But the space where I was to write my mother's name I left blank. Shortly after I handed my card to Mrs. "S", the music teacher, she asked me to come to her desk. My heart skipped for I figured I was in trouble. She told me I had forgotten to put in my mother's name. Tears welled in my eyes. I stammered, "I do not have a mother, she died." I looked up at Mrs. "S" and there were tears in her eyes.

From that day forward she took me on as her special project with private lessons all the way through High School and small jobs for her on weekends to keep me busy. Her love filled a great void in my heart. My love for her lasted for decades as she came to know my wife and kids. I was progressing with my violin and soon became her prize pupil and the "star" of all her recitals. I went on to play in all my school orchestras and even tried out for Seattle's Youth Symphony before I went into the Navy. I once was the solo violinist for the World Missions Conference at Seattle Pacific University. She was there. I was very nervous. She told me to look at her at the piano just before I begin to play. I saw her mouth the words "you can do it." It was one of the first assurances that God could use a damaged youth like me. My violin now rests on the shelf above the fireplace, mounted beautifully by one of our sons. We remained life-long friends. She later was delighted with Marilyn and our boys. There were other "angels" too.

PRINCIPALS CAN BE ANGELS TOO

Junior High School was difficult except for orchestra and one other surprising event. I think P.E. (Physical Education) was the hardest on me although as it turned out I became a good athlete. However, in junior high I could not hit a baseball for anything. Later I learned that I needed glasses. In those days the coach would pick the two best boys to be team captains Then the captains would choose who they wanted on their team.

Needless to say I was the last to be chosen and in my eyes the looser had to take me. I hated baseball. I was not good at basketball either due to a congenital heart condition which I found out as an adult. But when it came to tumbling (gymnastics), I exceeded to the best in the class. The baseball "jocks" did beat me up in the locker room once. Junior high was not all bust. I did well with my violin and became concert master of the orchestra. Every spring we had the big spring concert event. It was my time to shine. I always wished my father would attend the concert. However, he worked hard and never went out in the evening as he had to get up early for work. One year there he was in the front row proudly watching me perform. I had to really concentrate on the music especially during the ballet dances so I would make my Dad proud. That day I did make him proud even though one of the strings on my violin broke and I had to wait for an intermission to replace it. After that we did a lot of things together. We spent many a Sunday afternoon at the zoo or riding horses or going to the beach for a picnic. He was bald and one day he was sleeping on the beach when a sea gull mistook his bald head for a rock and dropped a clam shell on his head. Sea gulls do that to break open the shell. The shell did not break, but it cut Dad's head. I never saw him jump up so fast. We would fish and sometimes the sea gulls would dive down and grab our catch in their beaks and fly away. So I derived the idea of tossing a large lighted firecracker in the air to scare them off. It worked, but only after one bird caught the firecracker in his beak and it blew his head off. I never did that again.

One day a buddy suggested I run for treasurer of the school's Boys Club. Me? I did not know anything about "politics" and I was sure that I was not a good speaker for the campaign. But I had help writing my campaign speeches and when it was all over I lost by less than ten votes.

I graduated from junior high and moved on to West Seattle High School. It was then that my brother returned from the war. He had been a ball turret gunner on a B-17 bomber flying many bombing raids over Nazi Germany. The war was over. I was in wood shop class and happened to look up at the window in the door. There was Lester's face smiling at me. I made a bee-line for the door. Les had gotten permission to take me out of school that day. We went home and talked for hours. I wanted to hear all about his adventures, but he was reluctant to talk about them.

We had all earlier joined the West Side Presbyterian Church which had a great youth program. My best friend was going to Seattle Christian School where his father was principal. One day he suggested that I transfer to Seattle Christian. I had a good paper route and did lawn mowing in the summer which paid the tuition. So I started some of the best years of my school life there.

Moving to a smaller, Christian school gave me opportunity to develop my personal skills. Of course I joined the orchestra and was soon its prize member. I sang in the choir and we formed a boy's quartet which gave concerts in various churches helping to raise money for the school. My friend and I were two of a kind often giving his dad concern because we were in the midst of it. We both played on the football team He was quarterback and I was a wide receiver. I was very fast and was able to outrun most tacklers.

His father, the principal, was different than any other principal I knew. He was very involved with the students. He was coach, teacher, disciplinarian and friend. I remember going rabbit hunting, skiing, and other fun things with him. When the State Fair was in session he would take the whole school to see it. One day the Barnum and Bailey circus came to a lot next to the school. They asked for high school boys to help put up the huge tents. We were to receive free tickets to the circus. We worked all day under those dirty tents. We would push up hard so the elephant following us could get his trunk and head under and raise the tent. It was great fun. However, the circus refused to give us our tickets, so our principal went over and soon got them. One day we went rabbit hunting on Whidbey Island. He took his daughter with us. She was the only girl. We were eating lunch sitting on a log when the log rolled and we fell off. Everyone blamed her of course only to find out later it was a mild earthquake that rolled the log.

One of my other close friends was great at baseball and went on to play semi-pro baseball. Between the school and church I had many friends There were summer camps, hiking trips, skiing, and lots of fun. We remain friends to this day.

We had a great lady teacher in the school. She taught in the high school in most everything and she, too, was a great friend. Since there were no women in my home at that time she taught me how to treat a lady, walking always on the street side, opening doors etc. She was also a good ping pong player and a great shot with a twenty-two rifle. We would bury a bullet in a huge stump and she could fire it by hitting it with a bee-bee gun. No one could beat her at ping-pong. It was soon understood that we were not just students, but loved by the staff. I kept in touch with her even through the years in Japan where she visited us once, and by letter the years she taught in China. We corresponded every Christmas until the last couple years. I am sure she has passed away by now.

Becoming Student Body President was a great honor for me as well as singing tenor in our quartet. In this small school I became popular. Yet deep inside there was that hidden dungeon of pain that I would not let surface.

Just a few years ago I was visiting my brother in Seattle. He and his wife went to a wedding one afternoon. Since I did not know the couple I stayed behind. As I sat on the davenport I wondered if my former principal still lived where he did in West Seattle. Looking in the phone book I found that he did and gave them a call. His wife answered. She used to have students over for great clam bakes. We would gather the clams and she would boil them in a big wash tub, dip them in bread crumbs and fry them a little. Then we would have clam eating contests. Her son always won. Anyway, she invited me over. Greeting me at the door she brought me into the very familiar home. My friend, the principal, was sitting in a wheel chair with tubes in his nose and throat. He had difficulty breathing. For over an hour I related to him all that he and the school meant to me and how much I loved him for it. It was a great reunion. I said I would call again the next day. I did so and found that he had passed away shortly after I had left. I was encouraged by God's timing in reminding me of him so I could see him before he passed.

When I was fifteen my father remarried. Betty had been my mother's best friend. Her husband had passed away not long after my mother did. My brother, along with Betty's children, pushed Dad to pursue a relationship with Betty. He went to Spokane to see her now and again and soon got up enough nerve to propose. I was Best Man at their wedding. Since I had known Betty most of my life, I soon called her "Mom". She loved me as my mother did and I was delighted. Since Seattle Christian was not accredited at that time I had to take my last semester at Garfield High School. I only had a couple of classes so I turned out for track. It was then I realized how fast I was. My first one hundred meter race I won matching the school record. I was a shoe-in. However, Betty had lost her 17 year old son to a heart attack so she asked me not to run with the track team. I learned later about my own heart condition and now see her wisdom in that decision. I obeyed, of course.

Missionaries had always intrigued me. One Sunday morning at church a special missionary lady from China spoke. I remember she had a quart jar of string beans which she ate with chop-sticks. Her name was Ms. Julia. It was then that I knew I wanted to go to the orient as a missionary. That "call" remained throughout our years as missionaries to Japan. On a furlough from Japan I was speaking at the same church and related the story of my "call" to Japan. After the service I was shaking hands at the door when a little old lady with a glowing face took my hand and squeezed it hard. "I'm Ms Julia", she said. Of course hugs were in order.

In the High School boys Sunday School class as a teen at that church I earned a beautiful Bible by memorizing the entire Westminster Shorter Catechism. There were one hundred seven theological questions with the answers. It was a real task, but I succeeded. The first question is:

Q "What is the chief end of man?"
A "Man's chief end is to glorify God and enjoy Him forever."

That theological grounding gave me great comfort the rest of my life. I saw it demonstrated through my principal at Seattle Christian High School. One day a gentleman came into the school in the front hall began a railing against him. He was angry because the school did not hold to his extreme theological view. The principal did not answer in a tone of angry response, but kindly expressed his concern over the issue and reiterated the school's theological position. He did not raise his voice, but stuck to his principles. Since the protester did not get anywhere he turned and stomped out the door. Yes, principals can be angels too.

CHAPTER THREE

"SEMPER FI"

TAKING ORDERS

It was called the "Forgotten War". The Korean War was the first of the unpopular wars. It was called everything from a "police action" to simply a regional conflict. Hatred was not thrown upon us when we returned like it was in the Vietnam War. We were just ignored. The Veteran's Korean Memorial was built long after the Vietnam Veterans Memorial in Washington D.C.

I had just turned eighteen when I joined the Naval Reserve, hoping to get some college under my belt before I got called up. I talked it over with Dad and Mom. Dad had been in the infantry in France at the end of WWI. He was a military police officer in Paris. He jokingly said to me, "Son, join the Navy and stay out of the infantry." Little did I know then where that decision would lead me. I only got one semester at Seattle Pacific College in Seattle when I received my orders to active service in the U.S. Navy. I arrived in San Diego for basic training. As typical snafus are, my medical records did not follow me, so I endured a fresh set of shots even though my arms were red and swollen from the first. It was soon revealed that I had been a pre-med student at SPU. So I was assigned to the Hospital Corps School in Bainbridge, Maryland where I exceeded in classes like combat minor surgery. Following graduation I was sent to the Naval Hospital in Newport, Rhode Island for my internship training. I enjoyed the Navy and the responsibility the hospital training afforded me. The Navy routine and discipline was exactly what I needed in my young life

In boot camp one day as usual we were up by five a.m. and out on the grinder, the large concrete assembly area. all lined up for inspection as the chief passed by. When he got to me he yelled, "Sailor, pick up that butt." "But, sir, I don't smoke and didn't put it there." Big mistake. Well, I picked up the butt and spent the rest of the day with a bucket of water and several tooth brushes scrubbing the grinder. I learned a valuable lesson about obeying what your superiors said. It would serve me well later.

Being on the East Coast I dreamed about perhaps being assigned to the Naval Hospital in Naples, Italy. So much for that. After a few months at the Naval Hospital in Newport, I received orders to the Fleet Marine Force, Pacific Command. Off to Camp Pendleton, California I went to join the Third Marine Division soon to deploy to Japan. This was an attempt to force the North Koreans and Chinese to agree to a cease fire. After a short time in Japan I was transferred to Korea and found myself at the front lines with the First Marine Division. As my transportation slowly moved me to the front we passed the ravages of war, bombed buildings, ragged, begging children, the whole bit.

Arriving at the Regimental Headquarters of the Fifth Marines, 1st Marine Division, FMF, north of the Imjim river we were met by the Regimental Commander. A Colonel, he instructed us on our duties on the front lines and assigned us to battalions and infantry companies. I was assigned to the Regimental Aid Station. I had my own jeep and driver as we made many trips "forward". There were pill boxes with machine guns, fox-holes and bunkers. Just to our rear was a Marine Artillery Company and further to our rear our field medical hospital, Able Med. Jumping into a fox hole one day I was reminded of my Dad's advice to join the Navy and stay out of the infantry and here I was with the toughest infantry outfit in the world. I wrote him and chided him of his "poor" advice. It was shortly after the truce so I was not in immediate danger, though some fire fights did occur. Here again I saw God's grace over the long run. We were stationed at the foot of Hill 229 with the hill just north of us being the front line of our forces. Between us and the enemy was the demilitarized zone. It was essential that we kept our eyes peeled as the "gooks," as we called the enemy, often came across under cover of night and through tunnels to spy and get in behind us. This was against the truce, but our side did the same thing. We were ordered not to shoot anyone we caught crossing into our defenses as we would not know whether they were enemy or foe.

George Pontius

THE GOOK CEMETERY

I was on duty at the Regimental Aid Station when the field phone rang making me jump. It was the 2nd Battalion's aid station. They had a casualty, a DOA that needed to be transported back to our Regimental Aid Station. We needed to come and take care of it. I grabbed my driver, hopped into the jeep and headed north. On the way we passed what appeared to be a very new cemetery with dozens of graves. My driver informed me that it was the Gook cemetery. A strong breeze was blowing making the rusting cans and metal shards groan as they hung on the barbed wire. A destroyed village was next to the cemetery which accounted for the graves. I turned and said "It doesn't make any difference does it?" "What doesn't? You OK, Doc?" my driver asked. "Yah, I'm OK," I replied. "Somewhere in South Korea, North Korea or China a mother is crying for her loved one. It really doesn't matter, then does it? Death is the great leveler of all men," I said. Silence pursued us as we both wiped a tear from our eyes.

When we arrived at the 2nd Battalion a chopper was landing to take the body back behind the lines. The young corporal had killed himself with his 45 pistol. The bullet had entered his chest and blown out his entire back. He had been to mail call every day and never got a letter. He also had a big problem with his boots which were too small. Military supply lines were very slow and his new boots had not arrived. In lonely desperation he ended his life. He had survived the last six months of the war where the fighting had been very hard. Yet, loneliness and depression had done what an enemy bullet did not. Having finished what we came to do we returned to our jeep. No words were spoken. We both hurt for this lost kid. War is mankind at its worst on both sides, some just worse than others.

Later, I don't know when, there appeared a poem in the Stars and Stripes written by a Navy Corpsman about 1953-'54, maybe earlier. It was unsigned. It speaks for itself and for all Navy Corpsmen and all medics in every war.

OF SILENT BATTLEFIELD

Now the cannon has stopped its throaty roar...bearing forth its searing
> Projectile fruit,

Frayed bits of cloth...fluttering in the wind on barbs... are faded.

Junk...it's all junk...the wheel of a jeep lying half covered in the rutted
> blacked earth...a piece of cartridge belt hanging

on
> A bare scrub.

The cold has made the earth hard again.

Beneath its pock-marked crust...lie those who have listened in silence.

Before me is the battle...how many hours, weeks...ago?

Sprawling...encompassing all.

Rust creeps with its steady sureness over fragments of steel...that have
> returned themselves to the earth.

The war steel...of helmets and planes...of tanks and the dog tags,

No...dog tags do not rust.

This part of war steel...the faithful markers do not rust.

Wind...blow high...over the gutted hillsides and hilltops.

Voices I hear you bring...of rifleman...BAR man... planter...
> patrol leader...soldier in the hill.

Blow stronger wind...I hear them clearer.

Scraping voices...hoarse...faint on the rice...strong young voices...
> old tired voices.

Shouting, crying...whispering...praying,

Battle...oh battle...savage, tearing....devouring the young faces.

Making them anonymous in the earth.

Who weeps here...with heavy salty tear...to water the crusted graves?

Come...come wind, and tell me of those who trod once... and now lie
        here.

Bring to me the sound of river blood...gurgling and seeping...absorbing
        into the earth.

What can I hear now, after this...lullabies of Mothers'... the cooing of
        doves...Broadway on a Saturday night...voices in alma
        mater...what I can hear now?

You there...down in the earth...what do you hear?

You, with wrists in wire bound tight.

The sound of foreign tongue...the metallic click of weapons...of your
        deaths?

Let 'em reach gently...gently...and snip these bonds that you may
        ly with outstretched arms...feeling of your world down
        there.

How much of a journey have you traveled...from the
        spit-shine in basic?

What paths have led you here...under?

Is it you that radiate this cold to the crust above you?

Brother...brother...how many tears can I give?

RECKLESS

It was then I met Reckless, later to be immortalized in Andrew Geer's book, *Reckless, Pride Of The Marines*. She was a corporal when I met her. By the way, did I mention that she was the foul of a Japanese race horse? Reckless belonged to the 4.2 mortar company, and had been used very effectively to carry ammunition up to the top of the hill where the recoilless rifle emplacements were. She was loved by all of us in the 5th Marines. One day our guys managed to hide her for ransom. Tickets were sold for one dollar each and the money raised went to the Marine Corps Widows Fund. In our regimental headquarters battalion a lot of money was raised before her owners found out where she was. One day Reckless got into some 30 caliber ammunition and tried to eat several clips damaging her teeth. So she went to sick-bay to get her mouth repaired. The doctor examined her and one of the corpsmen used a hydrometer borrowed from the motor pool to wash out her mouth with saline solution. It was time for a photo which is now in my Korean War album at the Naval and Seas Services Museum in Spokane, Washington.

RECKLESS, PRIDE OF THE MARINES

Taken by R. George Pontius USNR
5th Marines 1954

We made a beach landing exercise some time after the truce. Reckless stayed behind. When we were climbing down the nets from the troop ship to the LCVP bobbing heavily in the rough seas I realized that I had to time my jump from the net to the landing craft just right to keep from being injured. I was in the third wave to hit the beach. We were packed so tightly in the boat that each man had to help the man if front to get his M1 rifle from his back into his hands to be ready when the boat hit the shore and the front ramp dropped, rifles with bayonets fixed at the ready.

We hit the beach, the ramp dropped and we rushed out into the water and onto the beach. We "secured" the beach and headed for the trees where we dug in. That night flares lit the sky and there was a loud scream…"doc.. doc!!" I grabbed my medical pack and rushed toward the scene. A marine was on his back in a fox hole, his back sizzling from the horrible burning of a flare that had landed on him. Other marines brushed the flare off and we smothered the flames, got him out and began dressing his wound. The smell of burnt flesh was nauseating. He was evacuated by helicopter. It was a Bell copter with a stretcher on each landing strut. On one such occasion the pilot had not brought sandbags for ballast, I was placed in on the other stretcher. It was quite a ride being outside the chopper. We landed at our field hospital. I was returned by jeep to my unit.

One day some time after the truce Reckless once again proved herself to be very smart. Orders were that no one, absolutely no one was to ride Reckless. However, headstrong buck sergeant decided to do just that. Bareback he kicked her into a fast run. However, he was headed right for a live mine field, marked with wire and red flags. We were all yelling at him to stop. He kept going, but Reckless had other ideas and suddenly stopped short of the mine field throwing the sergeant over her head onto the ground. The next day he was reduced in rank to corporal. Reckless liked to come into the tents on cold nights. The tents were lined with parachutes to give some insulation. It was very cold that winter. She would lie down between the cots, her body providing some welcome warmth. After I was rotated home with the last combat rotation Reckless made officer rank, and eventually was shipped back to Camp Pendleton where she advanced in rank and finally died, a real Marine hero of the 1st Marine Division.

CHRISTIAN FRIENDS

When I first left home for the Navy I asked the Lord for some fellow sailors who would be good Christian friends. At every duty station I always found some. Upon arriving at the 5th Marine Regiment I was assigned to the Regimental Aid Station. As I entered the door to the station I saw another corpsman sitting on a stretcher. He was holding cards in his hand and moving his lips as he looked away from them. I recognized the cards as the Navigator's Scripture Memorization Cards. "I see you're memorizing Scripture," I said. His name was John and we began a fast friendship that has remained for over fifty years. He soon introduced me to the Regimental Chaplain. It was not long before I was playing the piano for all chapel services. I was not much of a pianist as I played mostly by ear, but I was all they had. So every Sunday I would listen to the same sermon ten times. The first was at our regimental service and the other nine in bunkers that stretched across the front line along the demilitarized zone (DMZ). The chaplain and I would take his jeep and go along the ridge from bunker to bunker carrying a portable folding organ. Anywhere along the line of bunkers we could gather a few marines we would hold a service. Soon we had morning Bible studies at the regimental headquarters.

There were four or five of us involved in the chapel services who had not been baptized. So Easter Sunday afternoon we five and the Chaplain rode down to a clear spot on the north shore of the Imjim river near the Libby Bridge. There we sat up a crude altar on a half-sunken, bombed out tank. We were then all baptized in the Injim river. It was a deeply humbling time for all of us.

We were at corps reserve when some marine buddies remarked, "Man it's hot and muggy today, let's go to the slop-chute (a crude home-made bar in the camp). I had never before drunk a beer or anything like it. However, since beer was the only cold drink I decided to have a beer. Soon one led to another and as my marine "buddies" urged me on I chug-a-lugged a few and became very drunk. I almost immediately became violently ill and vomited for several hours. Fortunately for me it prevented alcohol poisoning and a bad outcome. The next morning I was still blurry-eyed and sick. The chaplain sent me back to my bunk with a disappointed glare. I never drank again. It took a long time to regain my testimony for the Lord.

One day at corps reserve a loud shout of " "Hit the dirt" came from the nearby ammunition depot followed by rifle fire. Some gooks had almost gotten to the area planning to blow up the dump. Guards spotted them and a lively fire-fight ensued. It was then I remembered my boot camp Chief teaching me to obey orders, not to question them. I jumped into a nearby fox hole until it was all over. The top sergeant in our combat field training at Camp Pendleton told us not try to figure out the enemy, just listen to our sergeant and company commander who knows the enemy better than we did. It is a good plan for Christian soldiers also to listen to the Holy Spirit rather than ourselves.

It was a nice sunny day when we learned we were going home. The last combat draft was being rotated back to the States after fourteen months in Korea. It was the fall of 1954. John and I were among those going home. We boarded an old train at the Freedom Gate Bridge. It was so named because it was where after the truce Chinese and North Korean soldiers who were defecting to Taiwan had crossed into United Nations hands. As our train neared Seoul it slowed. We opened the windows. Just outside were hundreds of children, arms outstretched for any candy or goodies we might give them. I noticed one little boy with a dirty face, ragged clothes and rubber shoes reaching up to me. He was no more than four years old. Tears streamed down his cheeks as he was too small to reach the many hands with candy extended to him. I pushed myself half-way out of the window and filled his little dirty hands as full as I could. He look up at me seeing the tears that were in my eye. How I wished I could have lifted him into my arms and taken him away from all the horror of war. To this day I think of him, wondering if he ever grew up, what he might be doing and where he is. These are the images you never forget.

Our troop ship sailed under the San Francisco Bay Bridge with fireboats shooting streams of water in welcome. There were no other signs of welcome home. We were bussed onto Treasure Island Naval Base for processing. John and I changed from our Marine uniforms back into our Navy Blues and went on liberty. It was a Sunday and we headed for the Japanese Gardens in San Francisco. Unknown to us John's very good friends, Don and Marguerite were in San Francisco from Los Angeles. They were the hosts of the Gospel Servicemen's Center in LA. Marguerite knew we had landed and she was anxiously looking for us. As we were coming up over the rise of the Japanese Garden bridge there they were coming from the opposite direction. Don later related how embarrassed he was because Marguerite stared at every sailor she saw hoping to recognize John. It was my first introduction to them though I had written to them from Korea. A long and lasting friendship followed which only ended upon their deaths.

John and I mustered out of the service together. Hoisting our sea bags onto our shoulders we headed to the train station and there said our goodbyes. The friendships welded on the battlefield are never forgotten. It would be over thirty-five years before we spoke again.

CHAPTER FOUR

PREPARATION FOR THE LORD'S SERVICE

HOME AT LAST

Home - how long had it been - over fifteen months? Mom and Dad hugged the dickens out of me. It was good to be home and ready for a new adventure. I soon got on the phone and contacted old friends and met new ones. My brother was the Presbyterian missionary to the Shoshone and Paiute nations on the Duck Valley Indian Reservation that borders northern Nevada and south Idaho. Owyhee, an old western town is just south of the Idaho border into Nevada. My father had purchased a new Plymouth while I was in Korea and I had been making payments on it. So with a nearly new car I drove the hundreds of miles to Owyhee. I intended to stay only the summer, so I had not packed that much. I was having to renew my wardrobe since I was back in civilian life and did not have much. Along the road south of Boise, Idaho toward Mountain Home was mostly desert. Frequently huge billboards would appear with the message, "Monotonous, Aint It?" They were put there by the Stinker Gas Stations. They surely brightened the otherwise dreary trip. The last one hundred miles was dirt and gravel. In the winter it was covered with snow as the elevation of Owyhee was about five thousand feet above sea level.

Pulling into town I thought of the old western towns I had seen in John Wayne movies, complete with a wooden sidewalk. The only difference was the Confectionary which was a kind of drug and ice cream store. There was no saloon but the general store had wooden swinging doors. A very old fashioned gas pump stood at the edge of the wooden sidewalk. There was one Shell gas station and repair shop. A fairly modern school was across the street next to the Presbyterian church where my brother was pastor. Competing with automobile traffic, horse-drawn buggies and buckboards moved slowly up and down the unpaved main street. On one side of the street an irrigation ditch flowed through town.

I saw the white church with its steeple and turned into the parking lot across the canal. Lester and his wife came running out of the mission parsonage to greet me. I think we talked the entire night before falling asleep exhausted. Les and I had not had such a time together since he was discharged from the Army Air Corps in 1945.It had been nine years.

THE CATTLE DRIVE

During the next few weeks I became acquainted with the great people of Owyhee and was eagerly accepted. I helped Ed with Boys Brigade which was a type of Christian Boy Scouts. He and his wife were Wycliffe Bible Translators on the reservation translating the Bible into the Paiute language. They lived in a house trailer in back of the manse. These boys who were eight to twelve years old reminded me of the children in Korea, but much better clothed and fed. When we went on campouts they could teach me more than I could teach them. Some of those boys went on to be great tribal leaders.

One day Lester asked if I would consider staying for a year and working with the children and young people. My plans were to go that September to Whitworth College in Spokane and begin my preparation for the Christian ministry. He urged me to stay stating that a year on the reservation would be a great addition to my ministerial preparation. However, there was one problem. How would I support myself?

I was becoming personally involved in the ministry at Owyhee. It pained me to think of leaving when the summer's over. I compromised saying I would stay through Christmas and then enter college at mid-term. Lester wrote the Board of National Missions of the Presbyterian Church asking if there were any funds for me. They said no, but gave permission for us to ask supporting churches to send help separately. That was my introduction to faith giving and faith living. We would be dependent on the Holy Spirit to supply our needs through those pledged to support us. It was a vital lesson learned because our entire missionary experience in the future would involve faith living. I was still not sure about going out on the limb of faith. At that time Ed, the Wycliffe missionary gave me an envelope. In it was a ten dollar bill which was a great deal of money for a missionary at that time. Also there was a slip of paper with this quote from the great spiritual leader, Andrew Murray. It read, "When you are most anxious to move is when you make the most pitiable mistakes." Also he included the Bible verse from Philippians 4:19, "But my God shall supply all your need according to His riches in Christ Jesus."

The letters of request for help from the churches involved were written and sent. Replies came from the four corners of America literally. We heard from churches in Seattle and Spokane, Washington, California, New England, and the South. They promised to send an offering every month. No amount was stated. I would just have to trust what the Lord said in Philippians 4:19 that He would supply.

I had been working with Ed in Boy's Brigade in meetings, campouts and other activities. Supplies were charged at the general store. The day to pay the bill arrived and still no money had arrived. I asked the proprietor to add up the amount. He presented me with a bill for $74.81. That was really a lot in those days. I said I would pay it as soon as possible. From there I went to the post office to get my mail. In the mail were three envelopes, one from three of the churches. My hand was shaking as I opened them and counted up the total. I could not believe it. Those five checks amounted to a total of $74.81. How could this be? None of the churches knew about the bill at the store. Then a thrill of joy hit my heart. Of course not, but the Holy Spirit did. Never again did I fail to trust the Lord's supply even in Japan when there were times when nothing was in the envelope.

Working with the teens, especially the boys, was difficult. They were seasoned cowboys and I a city slicker. Law enforcement on the reservation rested with one U.S. Marshal. When trouble came he would deputize others to help. One moonlit night there was a robbery at the Confectionery. The owner's nephew had broken in, beaten up his aunt and stolen a rifle and ammunition. He was now up in the old meteor crater that overlooked the town. His position gave him a perfect view of all the activity below. The Marshal knocked on our door as he had others and deputized us. We went across the street and hid in the shadow of the wooden walkway. The Marshall figured the robber's friends would supply him with food and drink. All liquor was forbidden on the reservation, but many seemed to have some of their own, or that which they had bought outside the reservation. My brother, I, the Marshal and one other person made up the four men hiding on the boardwalk. Just then a young man from next door to the Mission came up on the road. He was carrying a big jug on his shoulder. The Marshal figured that was whiskey for the young robber. He shouted, "Stop, this is the Marshal." He did not stop but ran throwing the jug into the canal. I, the youngest, took off in a dead run after him. I had turned out for track in high school and was fast. In just a minute or so I caught up to him and took him down with a flying tackle. The middle aged Marshal soon arrived and began kicking the young guy in the face and ribs with his pointed cowboy boots. I rushed at the marshal and pushed him off balance. "Why'd you do that?," the Marshal yelled at me, "he's just a dirty Indian." I was shocked at his attitude and yelled back, "he may be an Indian, but he is God's creation and you can not treat him that way." By then others had gathered and the Marshal arrested him and put him in the town's one room stone jail. I looked around and saw my brother wet and dirty coming toward us. He was carrying the whisky jug he had retrieved from the irrigation canal. I chuckled that the Parson, my brother, was the one who came up with the liquor.

Being a rural mission church we did not have an indoor toilet in the church. One had to take the path out back to the outhouse. The facility was in dire need of repair. Since one of my responsibilities as a Navy Corpsman with the Marines was to keep clean latrines I volunteered to dig a new outhouse. I got the creosote and potato sacks together with my trusty shovel. I spent a long time digging that hole to its required a six foot depth. I had not thought about a ladder to get out. The sides were very sandy and try as

I may I could not get a foothold. So I threw the shovel out of the hole and sat down in the corner to be rescued My sister-in-law saw the shovel come out of the hole and expected I would soon be in for lunch. Some time went by before she realized I had not appeared. The next thing I saw was her standing above looking down at me in the hole and laughing. That was embarrassing. However, what happened next was worse. Well satisfied that I had done a good job with the oil-soaked gunny sacks lining the hole I went to bed tired. The next morning the next door farmer was at the house telling me to get that **++ outhouse out of his grain field. It seems I had dug the thing too close to his irrigation ditch and when he turned the water on that morning it filled up and overflowed taking the outhouse with it and depositing it in his field. I still have not lived that one down.

Life on the reservation was difficult for many young men. We had more funerals in one year than I had ever been to before. There were a lot of tragic injuries and deaths that year, most of them among the young men. They drove their cars into the irrigation ditch and drowned, they had other accidents elsewhere, gunshot wounds and drunken fights. One such funeral introduced me to their ancient ways. My brother and wife were away from Owyhee and I was left alone in the parsonage. Late one night there was a knock on the door. I answered it to find an elderly chief all dressed in his fine feathers and beads. "Wife die, you come," he said turning and heading north toward the cemetery. I woke up Ed and we both drove to the cemetery. The grave had been dug and two-by-fours were placed over the hole with the pine box resting thereon. The old lady lay there in the casket dressed in her best native clothes. The Shaman, the local "witch" doctor, was also there. "Please give her a Christian burial," someone said. Ed and I looked at each other. Taking my Bible I read the Gospel story and gave an invitation to trust in Christ for salvation. A short prayer and then it was the Shaman's time. He muttered a few words in Shoshone which we did not understand and then placed rose briars in the casket next to the old women. These were thought to keep evil spirits away from the body. The lid was nailed on the coffin and it was lowered into the grave. The silence was overwhelming. Young men picked up shovels and began to fill the grave with dirt. The sound of the first thud of dirt on the wooden box sent chills up and down my spine. Soon the grave was covered leaving a mound of dirt the size of the coffin on top. Some laid flowers on the grave. Suddenly a shrieking cry of sorrow filled the air. The women threw themselves on top of the grave sobbing out their grief. All the way back to the mission compound and long into the night until dawn Ed and I could hear the wailing of sorrow floating over the breeze from the cemetery. Surely death without Christ is a terrible thing. My heart ached that my precious friends would find faith and peace in Christ.

Being only twenty two and fresh from the Korean war I thought I was invincible. Each Fourth of July the tribes would gather at what they called Fourth of July camp. Dances were performed in full regalia, drums sounded their perfect beat. There were gambling tents, lots of food and of course the movie area. My brother, Ed and I took a very big wooden "screen" to the campground. There we set up a projector and equipment to show Christian movies every night. It was my job the first summer to use the very old '30's flatbed truck to carry the large screen. The truck had four foot sides to it. Ed and I managed to get the screen into the truck with it leaning against one of the sides. Ed stayed behind and I drove off through the village toward the campground. Arriving there my brother asked me where the screen was. I looked back, no screen. Where on earth was it? I went back slowly covering every foot of ground from the campground to the church. Still no screen. We did not find it until the snow melted the next spring. Somehow it was lifted by a gust of wind and blown into the irrigation canal wedging itself under the large bridge to the school. No one could see it. The spring rains dislodged it and it was discovered sticking half out from under the bridge. The young cowboys teased me saying that it took a white man to lose a 12' X 12' wooden screen right in the middle of town and not be seen. I replied that it was the dust swirling from the road that made it invisible,

Since everyone wore cowboy cloths that was what I purchased upon arriving at Owyhee. Later that winter Lester had purchased a new car from his father-in-law. He asked me to take the bus back to Detroit, pick it up and drive it back to the reservation. Of course that sounded like fun. I boarded the bus and a couple days later arrived at the bus station in downtown Chicago. I was oblivious that my outfit looked strange there until a small boy tugged on my jeans, looked at my cowboy boots and western cowboy hat and said to me, "are you Roy Rogers?" I could feel the red creep up my cheeks and thought that every eye was upon me. "No," I replied, "I just live in cowboy country." I returned to Owyhee via Denver to visit my aunt and uncle. It was snowing and bitterly cold.

I could not get any heat into the car until one mechanic suggested I open the vents under the dash. I arrived home in Owyhee late in the night after fighting a blizzard for a hundred miles on the dirt road from Elko, Nevada to Owyhee. I was exhausted and glad to be home.

The summer before I left for Whitworth University Les said I was not yet fully one of the "boys". So I decided to join the roundup. Each summer the cattle were rounded up from their winter/spring range and driven to branding camp. It is a grueling ride for any seasoned cowboy. The young guys thought they would teach this city boy a lesson. They brought me the meanest horse they could find, failed to hook the chin strap correctly and left the saddle cinch loose. However, they did not know that I had spend my teen summers on my uncles' cattle ranch and was familiar with horses, cattle and roundup duties. So I took the reins, fixed the chinstrap, cinched the saddle tight and climbed aboard. Giving the pony a slap on the rump I galloped around the corral and stopped in front of the group. They were disappointed that they could not unseat me from the saddle. But, they had one more trick. They assigned me to riding strays. Now, that is a tough job for any young cowboy as it requires you to ride a lot more distance than the others. Cattle are notorious wanderers. They would stray to the right or left of the drive and it was my job to go get them and bring them back to the herd. Now, it had been over five years since I had been on a horse. I was one sore cowboy by the end of the day.

Branding camp is where they sort out the different brands into their own corral. The new calves have to be branded and the older ones dehorned and castrated. To do this in one quick operation the cattle are one by one driven into a narrow passage called the vice. When one is solidly in the vice the trap is sprung and the vice is closed holding them still. Then several cowboys would dehorn, brand and castrate all at once. My little pre-school niece yelled at me, "I'm going to tell its momma, uncle George." At branding camp the ladies would come down in a horse drawn chuck wagon and serve us meals. There was always a good potluck along with ground hogs on the fire and, of course, rocky mountain oysters. Those are the gonads from the castrated bulls. I did not like the ground hog as it was far too greasy for me.

Earlier that spring one of the boys took me hunting. I drove my car across a stream and dislodged the battery. There was no way it would start. I thought I should pray asking the Lord to get us out of the situation and my car back to town. It had been snowing and turned into a furious spring snow storm on that mountain. We built a fire, but soon it was clear we had to get off the mountain. We had not seen a single deer. So we took our rifles and what we could take with us and headed straight down the mountain. Arriving at the bottom we were at the edge of the raging Owyhee River with its spring run off. We had to cross that river somehow. Finding a beaver dam, we gingerly crossed, thigh deep in rushing water, with our rifles over our heads. Needless to say we got to the road on the other side sopping wet. We headed for town which was a long way off, trying to flag down a car as we walked. Of course no one would stop to pick up a couple guys who were now not only wet, but caked with mud from the dust of the road. Finally a station wagon stopped and let us ride on the tailgate into town. My sister-in-law could not believe the sight she saw at her door. The next day the garage repairman went up, fixed my car and got it back to town. The guys teased me about the prayer, until I explained that it was answered. "How? they sneered. "Well, I prayed that we would get off the mountain and home safely and also that my car would be returned to me. We are here and so is my car. Prayer answered.

Finally it did come time to leave the reservation. A girl my age was one of the helpers that came in the summer. We hit it off and were "going together." She lived in Yakima so she was riding with me home. It would be a long drive, but we thought we could make it in one day. The day we left the community held a "going away" party for us. They gave me a gift of well over one hundred dollars for the trip. That was a huge amount for them. We were really humbled by their love and generosity. Little did we know how much we would need every cent of it.

Earlier in the summer I had taken my sister-in-law for a drive out by the old Air Force emergency runway. We took my little niece along. Lester was not in town for some reason. We got lost and ran out of road. In the distance we could see the lights of a bunk house on the large ranch north of Owyhee. Setting off toward the light through an old wheat field we hit a rock and cut a hole in the oil pan. What to do? I decided to drive on even though it would no doubt ruin my car. It was dark and getting too cold to spend the night there. Finally arriving at the bunk house we woke up one of the wranglers and persuaded him to drive us to the main ranch house. There we borrowed a pick up with the promise to return the next morning for the car. It was about three or four in the morning when we got home. About nine the next morning I got Ed from his house and we drove in his 1939 Chrysler to the ranch. I returned the truck and we set off to find the car. It so happened that my car was out of gas. So we transferred enough gas from Ed's car to mine using a paper cup. It was really embarrassing. Eventually we got to the Shell Station repair shop where the owner, Mort, fixed the oil pan and filled the car with gas and very thick oil.

It was in this car that Marie and I started home. About a hundred or so miles out of Spokane we had just climbed a steep grade when the car blew a rod. The sound was terrible. All the way down the curving highway into Pendleton, Oregon we made such a racket that everyone knew we were coming. But that was as far as we were to get. The engine was ruined and we were stuck. It was late in the afternoon so we decided we better get a motel. Not being married we rented two rooms and had a warm dinner. The hundred dollars given to us had just paid for the gas so far and for our meals and rooms. That evening I called my uncle who owned the Buick Company in Spokane. Kindly he sent, at no charge to us, a tow truck with instructions to the driver to buy us steak dinners on the way home. Spokane was still hundred miles away.

Arriving in Spokane we stayed with my uncle and aunt while he put a new engine in my car. My aunt had a bright yellow Buick Roadmaster Convertible with leopard skin upholstery. It was the hottest car in town. My childhood friend, Donny, and his band were playing for a dance at the Coliseum downtown. As we drove into the parking lot in my aunt's bright yellow convertible all eyes were upon us. At last we had "arrived". We were the couple to be watched. I don't think anyone saw much as I could not dance and never have. But it was great fun

After the car was repaired I took Marie home to Yakima. Our engagement did not last long as I soon realized that she was not the one the Holy Spirit had chosen for me. The breakup hurt her, I am sure. However, finding the right girl was much more important.

That special girl was right there in Spokane all the time.

EXPERIMENT IN BLACK AND WHITE

The fall of 1955 I entered Whitworth College to begin my education.

As a ministerial student I took every Bible Course I could. Some really satisfied my hunger for God's Word, others didn't. One night I was asleep in my dorm room when there was a tremendous blast in the hall. I found myself under the bed with my arms over my ears remembering Korea. Soon I was aware of some younger students laughing in the doorway. I was furious that they thought my terror was funny. They never did it again There were other instances of youthful expression but I did not participate. Korea had mellowed me out quite a bit.

The next summer I worked for a local dairy which was owned by a long time friend from my church. It was at that time I met my future wife, Marilyn. I was boarding in the home of a high school friend whose brother was married to Marilyn's sister, Joan. Our first date was a blind date and a disaster. We were double dating with this friend and his girl. I had picked up Marilyn and we were on the way to pick up his girl. The first time I set eyes on Marilyn I was sure that was the girl for me. She did not have the same reaction. On the way we were rear-ended by some college boys who were looking for a fight. I turned the corner, stopped and got out to see what the matter was. Immediately they attacked me, ripping my watch off my arm and hitting me. I fell to the ground thinking that my friend would come to my rescue. That was not to be. He remained in the car "protecting the girls" he said. Soon the guys left and I got back in the car, not too damaged except for my ego. We arrived at his girls house only to find out that there was a phone call for me. My friend's mother knew where we were going. I answered the phone to hear the voice of Helen, my high school sweetheart. She informed me that she and her husband were in town and wanted to see me. We settled on a time. Then the two couples got back in the car. By this time I knew the date was a "bust." But we went on to Coer d' Alene, Idaho to begin our date. However, the place to which we were going was closed. We did grab a milkshake and returned home. I found out later that due to that bad first impression Marilyn was determined never to date me again. However, I would not give up. We were engaged three month's later and married the following June. It has been fifty three years now. Who says blind dates don't work?

In January 1957 I transferred to BIOLA College in Los Angeles. This great school began in Los Angeles at the Church of the Open Door at 6th and Hope street downtown. It was at that time the Bible Institute of Los Angeles (BIOLA). One of my best friends, Art, and his wife Donna were also there. Art and I walked into our first class late. It was the daily chapel service. We were at a loss for words. The entire student body was singing "To God Be The Glory." The song was new to me. The words and music sung by a thousand students reverberated form wall to ceiling and back again in that great old church. Classes were taught by the great men of the faith like, Dr. Sutherland, Dr. Talbot, and all others were filled with Biblical knowledge and truth. We both drank deeply from those spiritual wells. Later as seniors we were treated to a pancake breakfast by Dr, Sutherland. Every one of our professors had close relationships with us. I felt so at home and so free that I could go to any of them with any problem and find understanding, counsel and love. I indeed availed myself of their counsel and wisdom. I spent one year or so at the 6th and Hope campus. The sense of the Holy Spirit's presence permeated the place. Art and I remarked that we had to pinch ourselves to see if we had died and gone to heaven, so great was the spiritual atmosphere of BIOLA. Every student was required to have a "Christian Assignment". That was practical experience working in a church or other Christian ministries around the city. I chose West Adams Presbyterian Church were I was hired as Youth Director. The church was near the Coliseum football stadium on West Adams Avenue. Many of the members were from a gated community near by. There were a few black attendees also. The College group was all white, but the high school group was all black. It was a great time. A basketball court was set up next to the church and I spent a lot of time playing "horse" basketball with any youth that came by. Soon we had a good group. Marilyn taught piano to some of the group and I led the youth groups, both High School and College.

In the meantime Art was the youth director at a Baptist church in Culver City a few miles to the west of us. His youth were all white. One day we got our heads together and decided to combine the boys of our respective groups for a weekend campout. A member of our church owned a bus company and provided us with a bus and driver. We gathered at our church to board the bus. There were about twenty boys, ten from each church. Art's pastor was to be the vespers speaker. On the bus my black kids sat on side and Art's white kids on the other, by their choice. This was all prior to Dr. Martin Luther King and the civil rights movement.

The campground was somewhere out of San Diego by a quiet stream. Tents were erected and the camp was set up, black kids on one side, white kids on the other. It was difficult the first afternoon with little interaction between the two groups. That evening the speaker gave us the Gospel of love and unity, saying that we really were only one race, the human race. As the invitation to believe in Christ for salvation was given, both black and white guys stood together and prayed. By the end of the campout there was no division. I saw only "born-again" brothers inter-mingling and praying together. Christ can break down all barriers if we let Him. I guess we were ten years ahead of our time in terms of breaking the race barrier. Sadly, after we returned the relationships built faded mostly due to the distance between the two churches.

As our youth grew in Christ they asked to join the church. Pastor and I presented them to the session (council of elders) for membership. The room was silent for a short minute. One of the gated-community members rose to his feet and declared that no "n....r" was going to become a member of his church. All the other elders reacted in surprise. Both Pastor and I replied that if that was the attitude of the session we would resign immediately. Several spoke up, "Pastor, he does not speak for us." To which the gentleman retorted, " Well I give fifty percent of the money that comes to this church and what I say goes." "Sir", Pastor said, "then we don't need you. The Lord will supply." At that the rest of the session withdrew the hand-of-fellowship and dismissed him from the church on the basis of his defiance of the clear teaching of Scripture that everyone is welcome who trust Christ. The young men were accepted into membership and the next Sunday received by the congregation. God supplied the financial needs of the church. The experiment in black and white worked and God blessed.

THAT'S MORE LIKE IT

In high school when I had a girl my parents always got to meet her. My step-mother would look approvingly or disapprovingly. It was always with an approval and a smile. However, when I brought Marie home there was silence, She was slightly taller than I, but a lovely girl. When I brought Marilyn home to meet my parents there was a great smile and mom whispered in my ear, "that's more like it." I was amused but proud as well. The date for the wedding was June 14, 1957. While I was in California in school we wrote every day. There were times when I did not have enough money to buy stamps so I would still write and then send thirty letters on pay day. As the youth director at West Adams I receive only sixty five dollars a month. It never lasted long. I soon ran out of gas money. Being afraid to ask for help I would walk the five miles each way from the dorm to the church and back. On Sunday I would buy an apple and a banana for lunch and rest in the park nearby until the youth meeting in the evening. When my letters did not arrive each day Marilyn was worried that I had found someone else. Then all at once a bunch of letters would arrive and it was all right again.

School was out in late May and I headed home for the wedding. By that time I had a different car as I could not make the payments on the repair and traded my first in for an older one. It was a 1947 Chevrolet, brown with small windows. I stayed with my friend where I had boarded before and got ready for the big day.

It was a beautiful wedding which we preserved on 8mm film and tape. We still have it, but seldom get it out to watch. Marilyn was just beautiful as she came down the aisle. In my dorm room at BIOLA I had a beautiful framed, picture of her. Frequently the guys would see it and remark, "how can an ugly guy like you get a beautiful girl like her?" I often kept my door open so they could see my prize girl. In the basement of the church was the kitchen and dining room. Steps let up halfway to an outside door, turned and up another flight to the sanctuary. During the wedding the care taker felt he needed to get some of the big pots and pans out of the way. He was carrying them up the first flight of stairs to the outside door when he tripped and the pots and pans went tumbling and clanging down. It was all caught on audio tape, I had placed the microphone under the two steps to the platform out of sight. However, when we knelt on those stairs for the blessing it creaked and groaned like we were two old people. That was loudly recorded also. But we made it through and my beautiful bride and I were headed the next morning back to California.

The car was so packed that Marilyn sat in the middle next to me. Every other space was filled with our things and wedding gifts. Along the way we stopped to do some sightseeing. Marilyn's sister, husband and friends had painted the car with white shoe polish. It read, "Just married. Under new management." We never did get that off. We stopped at the big statue of Paul Bunyan in the Redwood forest. When we returned from the gift shop there was a large bouquet of wild flows and a note of congratulations on the windshield. Later we spent a day and a night in Sequoia National Park. For seventeen dollars we got a lovely cabin among the enormous trees, a nice dinner and breakfast. in the morning and it was on to Hollywood, California.

NEWLY WEDS

Our honeymoon was spent driving to California where I had a job in a dairy and Marilyn, a school teacher, needed to find a teaching position for the coming school year. Our first step upon arriving at Don and Marguerite's house in Hollywood was to find a place to live near West Adams Church. We stayed with our good friends for two weeks.

Finding a place to live was difficult. I was aware of the prejudice against African Americans even in the West in those days. So I was very clear that I was a youth pastor at an integrated church and we would most definitely be having all our youth group and other friends to our home no matter their race. Because of this we were frequently turned down. One such incident stands out in my memory. It was a nice apartment and in our price range. The owner was obviously a Jewish lady. When I told her that our black and oriental friends would be guests in our home she became very angry and told us that no black person would be allowed. As we left I wondered how a Jewish person whose people had suffered racial prejudice for so long, could be so racist.

Finally, we rented an apartment from a very strange lady. We had just purchased a slightly used Ford Thunderbird sedan. It was a neat car, white with red panel striping, white tires with red rims. Our landlady wanted us to park it out front as it looked like a police car in her eyes. We had to take the place unseen as the current tenant would not let us in to see it. Later we learned why. It was an upstairs apartment one bedroom, a small living room and a long hall back to the kitchenette and bathroom. Soon we were settled in our first home together.

Marilyn got a job teaching in the Watts district. I went back to school. My good friend, Art, and I were constantly together. After our morning classes at the college were over, we would take the lunch our wives had prepared, our homework and our surfboards to Playa Del Rey beach. There we would attempt to study in between hitting the waves. It was great! About four in the afternoon our wives would arrive with a picnic dinner and we continued to swim and surf, until the sun began to go down. Then it was back home, some more studying.

Before I brought my bride to Los Angeles I had a difficult time financially. The GI Bill paid my tuition, room, board and books. There was nothing left. The small salary from the church usually kept me in gas money. However, when I lived on campus the Bible College did not serve meals on weekends. So from Friday dinner until Monday morning I was on my own. I would save my money until about Saturday evening and then go to the corner store and buy a pint of milk and one banana. That had to last me until Monday morning breakfast. One Saturday afternoon I had just purchased my milk and banana and was waiting for the light to change so I could cross the street. Suddenly a taxi trying to beat the light, turn right, ran over the curb and knocked me down. My milk and banana flew out of my hands and under his wheels. There went my two day meal. I returned to the dorm dejected. The next morning, Sunday, I would have to walk the five miles to the church for Sunday School without eating since Friday lunch. I decided to go for a walk, As I was going down in the elevator the operator, a friendly little man, handed me one dollar. I asked him why? He told me that he promised the Lord that he would give a dollar to one student each weekend and that today it was to be me." It was the Lord's supply. I was able to buy a couple galloons of gas and a banana with that dollar. At another time Art and I were having coffee at our favorite restaurant. This place had a "grotto" in the basement. It contained a life-sized replica of the Garden of Gethsemane with Christ kneeling at a rock. A beautiful rendition of "One Solitary Life" was superbly read to a background of soft music. It was our favorite place to pray. We were just finishing our coffee in the restaurant when a lady at the next table stopped by and put a one dollar bill in front of each of us. "I promised the Lord that the first people I saw today who gave thanks before eating I would give them a dollar." She was another example of God's supply. This kind of evidence of God's grace were frequent though out our lives. I needed the humbling experience. His grace flowed to me through the Servicemen's Center and Don, the Director. They always had coffee and doughnuts which I could get there. I frequently assisted Don during services there. Now and then when I got back to the dorm I would find a five dollar bill stuffed in my pocket. Surely the Lord did supply all my needs, not wants, but needs.

Marilyn taught piano to some of the kids at church. One was an African American boy with huge hands. He could almost reach one and a half octaves. His feet were so big he had difficulty finding shoes. He asked Marilyn if she thought God could use such a big black boy as he? She assured him that God certainly could and that He would bless him in any ministry he undertook. We have often wondered where that precious child of God is today.

Our pastor's wife was up early every morning. She would wake us up, even on Saturday, with a phone call and "am I your alarm clock this morning?" She never learned that sometimes Marilyn liked to sleep in on a Saturday or in the summer.

Our landlady frequently made it clear that she would never allow a baby in the apartments again. Our neighbors had a baby and it cried now and then. We had indicated that we would stay at least a full year. However, friends of ours offered her father's house in Huntington Park for less rent than we were paying. We had not signed a lease but felt obligated to stay in the apartment. The Lord stepped in again. When the landlady said she would never allow another baby in the apartments, we informed her that we were pregnant and thus would be moving. We were anxious to move as she was an intrusive person, coming into our apartment when we were gone and snooping in every drawer. One time when we had gone home for Christmas Marilyn's mother had written cute little poems about the evils of snooping which we put in all the drawers. When we returned the landlady was very quiet and subdued. We knew she had read the notes.

At that time we owned only a TV and a coffee table. Marilyn's father bought us a crib for his first grandchild. We bought a piano and with the four pieces of furniture moved to Huntington Park. It was a large home all on the same floor with two bedrooms and a study "porch".

Our beautiful bouncing baby boy arrived in September 19th, 1958. We named him Steven Porter Pontius, the "Porter" after my father. Little did we know that we would lose him later.

THE PRISON

During the summer of 1958 I had been working for a creamery in Los Angeles. First in the freezer unit, then when summer was over I was asked to stay on and work nights in the steam-cleaning unit, There were ice cream bar machines and huge milk vats to be steam cleaned. This left little time for sleep or study. The only other person working the night shift was in charge of cleaning the milk vats. He and the foreman were good friends and they would leave half into the shift and go to a tavern and drink leaving the work to me. The rules were that neither of us could go home until both the vats and bar machine were cleaned. The conspiracy involved was to force overtime with overtime pay. I could use the money as Marilyn was not teaching with the new baby to care for and money was tight. I would go to work at three p.m. and often not get off until three a.m. Then I had a forty five minute drive home. I would grab three hours sleep, get up and study for an hour then head to school at BIOLA. Classes were over about noon. I would rush home and study for a couple hours before I had to be at work at three p. m. Needless to say it took a terrible toll on my health. The temperature in the freezer was about fifty degrees below zero and over one hundred degrees inside the milk vats when cleaning them. I was loosing consciousness doing that work. The doctor diagnosed it as severe asthma caused by the changes in temperature each night. He ordered me to quit my job right away as my health was in great danger. He wrote a note to the union boss and the management to that effect. The management was okay with the immediate work stop, but the union rep insisted I give two weeks notice. I could not, so I quit on the spot as the doctor had advised. I had previously mentioned to the management the alleged conspiracy. Thus the union rep had me banned for life from all union work anywhere in the USA. I could never work again in any union shop, so powerful was the union's power in those days.

Being quite ill at the time I was desperate to find employment that I could handle. Again I was to experience God's grace. The student employment office at BIOLA was aware of my need. Shortly I was called into the office. A position had opened up at the California Institution for Men at Chino, California. This was the famous "prison without walls". I applied for the job along with students from other seminaries and theological schools. I was only an undergraduate student in a Bible College but got the job. As it turned out the regular protestant chaplain was a Methodist minister who wanted the Gospel to be emphasized. I was his choice over the other more theologically liberal applicants. The pay was great and the work atmosphere wonderful. As it was a student intern position I was given a few hours with pay each day to study. It was a great experience preparing me for the pastoral ministry.

That year was very rewarding. I loved it at the prison, preaching, counseling and teaching Bible classes. It is my belief that every ministerial student should spend a year in such a position in a prison or jail ministry. Often we who have grown up in the church have little idea about the "real" world, especially the criminal one. We are ignorant of the tragic childhood that often brings a person to prison. The hurt, loneliness, despair, self-hatred, and anger that made up the lives of these inmates permeated most everything. Freedom was gone and hope was squashed. Their everyday lives were ruled by guards with night sticks and loud voices.

It was the responsibility divided among the three chaplains, Catholic, and Protestant to interview all inmates as much as possible and hold religious services and classes. Inmates were issued "chits" which permitted them to visit various areas of the prison. Thus the whereabouts of every prisoner was know to Central Control. Each shift my phone would ring and I would be given a list of inmates wanting to see me or whom I had requested.

Periodically the prison siren would sound and a full lock down instituted. Soon I would get a phone call from central control asking me to verify the presence of all men in my waiting room and office. When every inmate was accounted for the "all clear" was sounded and we would go back to our regular schedules.

Chino was a modern (1950's) experiment with no walls, only tall fences topped with barbed wire. There were no towers with guards, None of the guards carried firearms. This left the inmates free to wander at will or use the prison gym or swimming pool. Many trade classes were offered as well as an opportunity to complete high school. Their diplomas were issued by the local city high school. We chaplains were required to eat with the inmates at least one day a week. The rest of the meals were taken in the staff dining room. The food was great and the price cheap. At the south end of the compound was the "Reception and Guidance Center". Here three hundred newly sentenced prisoners were processed before moving to our main prison or San Quentin or any of the California state prisons. The average stay in the R & G Center was six weeks. We were supposed to interview these inmates also. It was beyond the ability of three chaplains to complete this task. So my responsibility at this high security section was to hold services and be available in case of an emergency. This might include counseling a distraught prisoner, or negotiating in a crisis. To be permitted in the high security building one would enter a barred door into a small cell. There he would state who he was, his staff ID number and his purpose. Then another gate was opened and he entered another cell. With the steel doors closed around him another door would open and a guard would enter to physically search for any weapons. Then the guard would leave and the final door would open and he was free to wander around the high security section.

One day I received a call from the warden asking me to meet him in the RGC building. After going through the security check I met with him in the main cell block. There were at least two tiers of cells surrounding an exercise area. It was explained that when the silverware was counted after the last meal a utensil was missing. This was a problem because it could be shaped into a weapon. With permission of the warden I told the inmates that if the offending item were to be thrown onto the exercise floor there would be no cell search. If not they would remain in lock down and every cell searched until it was found. The offending inmate would be charged with a further felony. After a moment or two of silence the knife clanged onto the floor and that was the end of that.

On another occasion I was summoned to counsel a distraught prisoner. He was a new inmate facing a thirty year term. The warden had just been notified that the prisoner's wife and entire family had been killed in an automobile accident. It was my job to inform him that it was impossible for him to go to the funeral at this stage of incarceration. It was a difficult time. I held him in my arms while he sobbed .and stayed for a few hours. He was then put on a suicide watch and I left. My heart was heavy with grief for him. What a waste of a young life! As I left the padded cell area I could still hear his sobs.

Easter Sunday came. I was to preach. I wanted music for that service other than the piano. We had a choir which was pretty good. We had no organist among the group, so I invited my wife Marilyn to come play. It was a disturbing experience for her. She brought our baby and laid his basket beside her. There were five hundred men filling the chapel. Marilyn was the only female. She could feel their eyes upon her. When the service began with singing all was fine. However, when I began my sermon Steven, our son, began to cry. There was no taking him outside the chapel so I tried to preach over his crying. Finally the service was completed and Marilyn and I returned to my office, then on home.

The next day I received a request for an interview. At each interview I would receive the prisoner's court records. Many of them were inches think. I would peruse what I could to get a background. But it was nearly hopeless as each interview was often confined to ten or fifteen minutes. A young man arrived and my secretary ushered him into my office. He soon revealed his reason for coming. "Chaplain, can a person start life all over again, like a little baby?" Of course I immediately led him to passages in John's Gospel about being "born again". He soon committed his life, past, present and future, to Christ the Savior. After praying with him I asked him what brought him there? "Was it my sermon yesterday?" As a young man vanity preceded that question. "No", he replied, "it was that crying baby. I remembered that I was once an innocent baby." Needless to say, my pride took a fall. I later told my son how God had used his crying to win a needy soul.

That year went all too fast. Hundreds of inmates came through my office. Many who became Christians were in my Bible classes. I have a plaque on the wall behind me from those inmates. It is still very special to me. That year

I experienced God's grace over and over both in my life and in the lives of many inmates. Some time later I had the pleasure of meeting some of them on the outside doing well some going to Bible college.

On my final Sunday one inmate embraced me and said "Chaplain, I may be physically in prison, but because of Jesus I am truly free" That says it all. "If any man be in Christ he is a new creation." 2 Corinthians 5"17 (NIV).

SURFING TO MINISTRY

During the final weeks at Chino we kept looking for another position. Checking the Jobs Available board at school I noticed that a small church in Costa Mesa, California was looking for a youth director. It would mean a move for us but BIOLA had just moved to its new campus at La Mirada, California near Anaheim. It would be closer to Costa Mesa than Huntington Park.

I interviewed for the position, laying out my philosophy of youth ministry and my theological position. I was definitely interested in reaching outside the church to draw youth who were interested. I wanted to teach the church kids to share their faith. This was a small Bible church affiliated with the Independent Fundamental Churches of America., known as IFCA. I was hired. The pay was only $300 a month. We knew it would be difficult even with my GI Bill as we were expecting our second child and have to supply some of the expenses of the ministry such as gas. We found a new apartment. It was not furnished. The first few nights we slept on the uncarpeted floor. This was very difficult for Marilyn as she was several months pregnant. We moved in with our TV, crib, piano and coffee table. Soon donated furniture arrived from the church members. It was pretty ragged, but it served the purpose.

When I got my working orders I was surprised to find that part of it was to take my surfboard and go to Newport Beach or Huntington Beach and see what I could find among the young people there. The plan was for me to take my equipment, surf and play with those on the beach. We gathered a small group including some of the church kids. One had a guitar, another a bass vile. Lighting a fire in the fire pit, we gathered around it and began to sing Christian choruses. It was not long before others would gather and listen. Always giving a short Gospel message we soon had a nice youth group of twenty or more at church. From that group great friendships were formed which remain to this day.

One of our first summer parties was a swim party at the home of one of the group. Unknown to me someone spiked the punch with liquor. It was not discovered until I felt dizzy and so did others. No one really got drunk, but for a very conservative church it could have been a disaster. I don't think any of the leaders found out as nothing was said. I made sure that never happened again. Our pastor knew because I told him and he was very understanding. He also became my mentor and friend for my life until his death a few years ago. We had a unique relationship. We agreed together from the first to support each other, to pray together and not to allow criticism to bring a wedge between us.

One by one these kids came to know the Lord as personal Savior. We attended a Christian Endeavor youth camp in the San Bernardino mountains called Tahquitz Pines. Each summer we took our youth group there. It held great times for us. I always went along as a camp counselor. One hot day many campers went hiking. A few stayed behind as I did to be staff members in camp. Suddenly a mountain thunder storm was upon us with thunder and lightning everywhere. Two boys were taking a shower when a bolt of lighting struck the power pole right outside the bath house. Immediately I saw two naked boys run out of the bath house screaming in terror. Fortunately there was no one except me to see them. I still laugh thinking about that scene.

One of our youth, Fred Martin, became close to us. He lived with his parents and many siblings in a one-room house. His parents had saved and were building a better house for them Freddie stuck to me like glue. One day he had just arrived to baby sit for us. We opened the door and handed Steve to him. Marilyn kissed Steve on the cheek. Steve pointed at Fred and said "kiss Fwed too" to which Fred replied, "ya, kiss Fwed too." You could always find Fred at the refreshment table at events stuffing his pockets full of cookies to take home. Fred later became the youth pastor of his home church, a pastor and hospital chaplain. Fred's father was a commercial fisherman and often brought us fish for for our dinner. We froze the tuna in a neighbor's freezer. With help of other members of the congregation we seemed to always have food on the table. Another member of the congregation took me deep sea fishing often. We would board a fishing boat early morning out of Newport Beach or Laguna Beach.

After six hours fishing I would bring home flounder, whitetail, and other fish. Our favorite was barracuda. This gentleman also provided us space in his freezer. Another gave us as crate full of cans of corned beef hash. During one low time we ate on the hash, one can for each meal, until it was gone. Never again have we eaten corned beef hash. However it was God's supply of our needs, not necessarily our wants.

Our Timothy was born at Hoag Memorial Hospital in Newport Beach. His nose was completely smashed over on the left side of his little face. It took a few days to straighten out. Just recently I received a call from one of his students at Cusick High School where Tim teaches to verify that story. Costa Mesa holds many great memories. There were campouts in state parks, spelunking, skiing in the mountains and of course days and days at the beach. Our youth group won every award possible in contests with other churches in Christian Endeavor.

It was during our first weeks in Costa Mesa that I had my first confrontation with demonic forces. We were asleep on the hard tile floor of our first apartment there when I felt a terrible oppressive *presence*. I immediately awoke unable to breath as I felt my throat being choked. I remembered the power of the name of Jesus and struggled to whisper "in the name of Jesus Christ leave me." Immediately the *presence* was gone and I could breath. In the morning I told Marilyn about it. She had not awakened as I thought she might. Together we went to relate the experience to my theology professor at BIOLA.

He had been a missionary in China and had experienced the same kind of oppression. He asked "did you make any kind of decision about the mission field recently?" I told him that we had received our appointment to Japan from our mission organization, New Life League. "That's it," he replied, He told us that Satan had sent his emissaries because we were planning to invade his territory. "Expect many such attacks from now on. You are marked," he told us. Later in a class on the Book of the Revelation the professor gave us some excellent advice, "Do not relegate the power of the Holy Spirit or the power of Satan to the first century." I never forgot those words. The Name of Jesus Christ remains our weapon of choice to this day in our spiritual battles. We were able to rent a house two doors from the church. There we bought new furniture cheap as it was, but sufficient.

I graduated from BIOLA College the spring of 1961. We were the first class to graduate from the new campus of BIOLA College. That summer I was ordained to the Gospel Ministry by the IFCA. Professors from BIOLA and many local pastors were the examining committee. It was a grueling four hour examination. Hours beforehand was spent with the written portions, including a translation from New Testament Greek to English. Because I was not a seminary graduate the exam was tougher than most seminary grads endured. The ordination service was held the following Sunday with ten local pastors participating.

Soon it was time to leave Central Bible Church for our important deputation. This is when independent mission organizations have their missionaries present themselves to numerous churches, organizations and individuals to raise support in prayer and finances for the work on the mission field. How would we tell our young people whom we had come to love over the past two years that we were leaving?

We had a missions trip planned to Mexico. This was the second of two trips we made to Santo Domino, seven miles from Ensenada, Mexico on the Baja peninsula. We had been building a small church in the village, making the bricks ourselves and placing them in place. Other churches were involved also. We decided since our replacement was with us, that we would tell them there. On this trip we took a battery operated megaphone. The village had no electricity. This would serve to draw villagers to the services and provide for amplification in the church. As we neared the village we climbed a hill nearby. The local lay pastor lived in a mud hut at the foot of the hill. Using the megaphone we announced our presence by calling Pastor Garcia's name. Suddenly the pastor rushed from his house and fell face down on the ground. We had not realized what this "voice from heaven" might sound like to him. Soon we set the record straight and entered the village. During our stay there we took our group of about twenty a short walk to the cemetery. It was very old. Sitting on the stone wall around the cemetery we asked the kids, "whose responsibility was it to tell these people about Christ?" Of course the answer was those Christians living at the time. "Then whose responsibility is it to tell others of Christ today?" The answer was obvious - those of us who live today. Then we revealed that we were leaving to go to Japan to tell the youth of Japan about Christ. Fred immediately got up and ran back to the village in tears. He was about fourteen at the time.

The new youth pastor introduced himself. But things would not be the same for Fred. It was two years before he transferred his loyalty to the new leader.

This was the most difficult time of our ministry so far. We would find that leaving other believers behind as we moved from place to place would be equally emotional. I never returned to Santo Domingo, but did return to Newport Beach and Costa Mesa several times. Memories are still vivid and clear. A portion of our hearts will always be there. Now and then we hear from those kids and their parents. Fred, however, is still our "son in the Lord" and always close in our hearts.

IN MEMORY OF GABRELLA RAMOS

September 6, 1997

(Written for her funeral)

I write this with mixed emotions. My eyes are filled with tears of loss for my dear friend and sister in the Lord. My heart rejoices to think of her now in the presence of her Lord and Savior, enjoying all the blessings promised the believer by Grace through faith. The Apostle Paul captures what I would say to Gabriella if I could. He writes in Philippians 1:3-6 (NIV) "I thank God every time I remember you. In all my prayers for you, I always pray with joy because of your partnership in the gospel from the first day until now, being confident of this, that He who began this work in you will carry it on to completion until the day of Christ Jesus." Dear Gabriella, His glorious work in you is now completed. What a glorious thought! I was only a wet-behind-the-ears ministerial student when I first met Gabriella and her family. Central Bible Church of Costa Mesa had hired me as their youth director. There I met life-long friends, sisters and brothers in the Lord, that continue to this day. Gabriella and her family were among those friends. We remember her holding our new-born son, Timothy, in her arms in the church nursery, cooing over him as he smiled up at her.

The last time I was in Costa Mesa was several years ago and as always made sure we visited the Ramos family. Gabriella had a lasting effect upon our youth group there. Her own kids were part of the group and she was involved. The Martins, Gablers, Wrights, the Beardsleys, Bob and Doris, Dal Spook and many others are all among our fond memories. It was Gabriella's brother who was lay pastor in Santo Domingo, Mexico. Through Gabriella, who was the spear head, inspiration and resource, we arranged the several trips we made to help build the little church in the village. Her brother taught us how to make adobe bricks from scratch and when the bricks had dried how to put them together to slowly construct that little church. Youth from a Methodist church in Orange County came down on different weeks than we did. We held meetings in a brush lean-to which served as a pulpit area. Many came to Christ. I wept over our riches and their poverty. We played baseball with the Mexican kids. They beat us royally and with great delight. On one trip we brought a truck load of clothing, food and other things for them Among the clothing there were several pairs of shoes. We searched for the right size for Pastor Garcia. He was delighted. The next morning he was not wearing them. "I can not wear them until everyone in my village has shoes." He really had a pastor's heart.

Marilyn and I wish you all well We pray for your comfort in the Holy Spirit. I pray for the joy of knowing that Gabriella is with he Lord today.

Pastor George and Marilyn Pontius

CHAPTER FIVE

"Honey We're Home"

GOOD BYE

Several months of hurried deputation left us tired and anxious. During this time in addition to pledges of financial support we were given a variety of items for the move to Japan. From several mission showers we received clothes, linens, lengths of fabric, and several other interesting gifts. Among them were dozens of safety razors. It was puzzling why someone would supply us with so many razors. Later it was abundantly clear that they would be desperately needed. We had raised the minimum monthly support of $300 but we were still short about $2000 for outgoing funds such as plane tickets for the family and other expenses along the way. Our departure was scheduled for two weeks away. With anticipation our home church, 4th Memorial Church, in Spokane was planning a farewell event. Children in the Sunday School had been filling Styrofoam cups with their offerings for weeks. Each cup had a picture of our family on it. A love offering had been announced that week and planned for our last Sunday. As I stood in the pulpit I looked at the stained glass window picturing Christ knocking at a door. It was the very picture I used to draw while sitting in adult church as a child. Wonder filled my heart that God's grace had brought us to that moment. I had much to learn about God's grace, mercy and love. I was about to earn my second big lesson.

Following the service we were dedicated to missionary service. All the children's mission cups were brought and an offering taken for our financial needs. A check was handed to us for the amount of almost $1500. God's fulfillment of His promise to supply all our need was still to come. With Marilyn and our two boys by my side we stood by the door to greet people as the service ended. Often something was placed in my hand or shoved into my pocket. It was a joyous but sad time. I had spent most of my life in this church and saying good bye brought tears to our eyes and a lump in our throats.. There were hugs from my former Sunday School teachers and many friends.

When we got back home to Marilyn's mother's house where we were staying, we laid the check and everything from our pockets on the table. We counted everything. It totaled $2100, one hundred more than we thought we needed. He indeed had supplied all our need and more.

That week we left for Seattle. I had previously taken all our barrels of goods to be shipped to Japan. We had given away everything we would not need in Japan, and put a few treasures in storage in my mother-in-law's attic. Marilyn's Mom went to Seattle with us to see us off. It would be a very emotional few days. Previously my father had suffered a massive stroke. He had recovered sufficiently to come to my brother's house where the family had gathered to bid us good bye. My Dad was too ill to go to the airport, so he and I were alone in the bedroom to say our own good byes.

Silence lingered like death before either of us could speak. We both knew we would never see each other alive again. Dad's days were limited and he would not survive the five years of our first term. "Dad," I hesitantly began, "how can I leave you here? Maybe we should stay and take care of you?" He motioned for me to sit beside him on the bed. His speech was slurred as he said, "Son," he began haltingly, "you must go. This is the day your mother and I planned for when you were born." He reached over and took my hand in his one good hand and continued, "I did not go into the ministry because of WWI and then I had to care for your grandmother. Son, your mother and I told the Lord that if He would give us sons we would dedicate them to His service. It was a great day when your brother was ordained and another when you were ordained. No I would rather die than delay your chosen ministry for the Lord." Silence again and tears with hugs. How does a son answer a father's prayer? I never saw him again.

The airport was crowded with people as we waited to board our plane for Japan There was another missionary couple boarding as well. We did not know them. Their family was gathered to say good bye. It seemed like ages of waiting. The family next door began to sing "I'll go where You want me to go..." I looked over at my step-mother, Betty, and saw tears flowing down her lovely cheek. Putting my arms around her, I held her tight. "I love you, Mom," I whispered in her ear. We would meet again.

We were so glad for modern air travel. In former days dockside goodbyes were permanent. The Boeing 737 was ready to board and our flight was called. "Northwest Flight #8 for Tokyo, Japan is ready for boarding" sounded over the airport speaker system. There were final hugs, kisses and good byes and we disappeared down the concourse. Soon Flight #8 slowly pulled away for it's docking. We could see our loved ones waving at the window. We waved back until they were out of sight, wiped the tears from our eyes and settled down for the flight to Japan via Alaska. As the big jet lifted off and banked out over the sea we knew our loved ones would stay by the window until we could be seen no more.

"HONEY, WE'RE HOME"

After seventeen hours chasing the sun we landed at Tokyo's Haneda International Airport. Going through customs we learned why the Lord had supplied the extra $100 as customs charges were just that amount. God knows our needs and supplies before we ourselves know. Waiting for us were a New Life League couple from Norway. The lady was very big and hugged Marilyn to her breast. She almost couldn't breath. We all crowded into a tiny Japanese car. It was about 3 a.m. I had been to Japan during my time in the Korean war. Marilyn had not. The sights and smells were strange to her. She squeezed my hand and whispered in my ear, "Honey, we're home." And truly we were. It was some distance to the mission compound. The roads had not all be repaired from the WWII bombings. Frequently we were jolted by a big chuck hole in the road and the boys cried out. Our driver knew the back roads as we passed through little villages. All of a sudden there was a loud bang and the car came to a sudden stop. We had blown a tire. Since it was early in the morning and most people were asleep our driver tried to be quiet as he checked the spare tire. But, there was no spare tire. Now what were we going to do with a carload of women and children? He soon found a car repair shop. It was shut up tight for the night. However, loud knocking and shouting at the door finally brought a response. A spare tire was obtained. However, we had no money with us to pay. So a passport was left to insure we would return to pay for the tire. We were fortunate that our driver spoke fluent Japanese. The sight of a tall foreigner at one's door was unsettling to say the least. The Lord was with us for sure.

We arrived at New Life League compound before anyone was up. Dr. Jarvis and his wife kindly loaned us a comfortable bedroom and suggested we get a couple hours of sleep. However, that was impossible as our boys had been sleeping most of the seventeen hours on the plane. Since they were only four and two years old trying to keep them quiet was a lost cause. We had nothing to entertain then with and no toys to play with. Marilyn and I also had slept many hours on the plane and were wide awake. It would take another three weeks before be got over our jet lag. But we were in Japan about to begin another phase of our lives. Yes, Honey, we are home.

THE COMPOUND

New Life League compound was near the Christian Academy in Kurume where many of the missionary kids went to school, some of them boarding there. The compound was in the early stages of building. We lived in a duplex American style house. Much of the work of the mission was in printing and publishing. It was the printing center for missionaries and Japanese churches and organizations. Later New Life League expanded to Sri Lanka, other oriental countries and Mexico. Our house was small but adequate. Since it had recently been erected some things were not yet installed. One of those was a hot water heater. To wash clothes or bathe we had to use a five gallon bucket. The bath room was typically a couple inches below the level of the other rooms. The tub was of lovely tile, but very large. Since we had to heat water on a two burner gas stove it was impossible to fill the tub with enough hot water before what was already poured in became cold. Thus the five-gallon bucket. To wash clothes Marilyn would fill the bucket kettle by kettle until there was enough water to wash. Our boys were two and four. The two year old took naps in a crib while Marilyn was washing clothes in the bucket. Tim managed for the first time to get out of the crib and come looking for "Mommy." The water in the bucket was extremely hot. Tim tripped over the ledge of the bathroom and fell his right arm going into the hot water clear to the shoulder. Marilyn screamed and I came running. Foolishly I ripped off his long sleeve shirt, and with it long strings of flesh. Immediately I wrapped his arm in a towel and called for our neighbor, Roy, to come. Roy got us into his Volkswagen bus and headed for the nearest U.S Armed Forces clinic. The road to the clinic was temporarily blocked by a Shinto festival and parade. Policemen whistled as Roy turned down the street anyway. The local god idol was on two poles carried by four nearly naked men who quickly moved out of the way as the dancers wiggled to the side, and we turned into the clinic compound.

Inside the doctor and nurses slowly removed the towel. We were shocked to see his little arm burned with strings of burnt skin hanging like cobwebs from a ceiling. Tim was given a shot for pain and the doctors began cutting and removing the damaged skin from his arm. All we could do was stand and watch reassuring Tim every time he called for us. One of the nurses pulled out a necklace she was wearing which contained a small music box. She held it in front of him while Tim played with it. Every time, which was daily for a while, we had to go back to the clinic Tim wanted to play with that music box.

We thought he would have a big scar but it was confined only to the back of his hand which was wrapped in huge bandages and hung to the floor. Steve watched over his little brother like a mother dog until he was completely healed

New Life League was completing the printing press building which over the years had many upgrades. Getting the press into the new building was quite an engerneering chore. We watched as the workers rolled the huge machine over poles and into the building. Soon it was printing in many different languages. Bibles in Chinese was one of the main jobs. Japanese sailors would sneak these into China as often as they could. We had at first planned to go on to Korea, but New Life League did not have work there so we stayed in Japan. I entered Japanese Language School in downtown Tokyo. Usually I road the train, but one day I bought a motorized bicycle. I decided to ride that to the Naganuma Language School. Traffic in Tokyo is horrific with cars going everywhere not obeying lanes or lane changes. I never did that again. Riding the train was also frightening at times. During the morning rush hour the coaches were so packed that my feet sometimes did not touch the floor. I was squeezed up by the crowd, my brief case held over my head. On the station platforms there were rows of shoes that had been ripped off in the rush to enter the train. Even the windows of the train on one trip shattered from the crush. When the train would stop at a station the mob pushing to get in would not let anyone off. The station police would use their feet to push the passengers in so the doors could shut behind them. Later when our boys went to the Christian Academy riding three trains the older ones would put their younger brother between them and the wall protecting him by holding their arms straight out from the wall to hold off the crush. On one such occasion when I was teaching English at a school in Shibuya downtown Tokyo, the crush was so great I began to panic and fought my way out before the train was any way near my station. I telephoned the school that I would not be there until the rush was over. It had been not a strike but a slowdown by train unions for higher pay. It was over in a couple days and things returned to their normal crowded ways.

That summer I was asked to be recreational director at a Japanese Bible Camp.

I was not prepared and it was an embarrassment. There, however, I met a young high School student. Masa was a great boy and I became his English tutor. Masa was baptized in his church in Yokohama. It was a joy to be there. Soon Masa became one of the family often visiting us over the weekend. Marilyn served oatmeal. The next time he came Masa begged that she not serve oatmeal. It made him gag. Soon Masa taught the children in our Sunday School. He graduated from university in Tokyo and was accepted to the University of Southern California, We arranged for him to live with friends from our church in Costa Mesa. Before he left we had Masa and his parents over for dinner. They had arranged a girl for him to marry whom he did not know. They wanted me to promise them that he would return and marry this girl. Secondly his mother wanted me to promise that there would be no earthquakes in California. It was a strange request as Japan is one of the most earthquake ridden nations. He arrived in California the day of a huge earthquake. I got an immediate phone call from his mother. Later he wrote that he had met the love of his life. They were married and now have two lovely daughters who are completely bi-lingual and trained in all things Japanese. It turned out that both "promises" were not kept. When the grandchildren came all was forgiven as his parents adored them. Masa and his wife, Janet, are now very successful architects involved with Disney World designs around the world.

It became evident that the desire of our hearts was not in printing but in evangelism. Further there were internal problems with the mission on the Japan field that led five families to withdraw. We were one of them. We moved to Karuizawa to go to TEAM Mission's language school. It was a difficult decision to make, but a wise one. The five families, after much prayer, formed a new mission which we called Japan Rural Evangelism Fellowship. We formed a Mission Board in the U. S. I will forever be grateful to Dr. Fred Jarvis and New Life League for giving us our start as missionaries. He is now with the Lord and New Life League is doing a great work for the Lord in many countries.

KARUIZAWA

Marilyn and I packed our panel truck, a "Cablite." with everything we owned and headed for the mountains one hundred miles west of Tokyo. The Evangelical Alliance Mission (TEAM) operated a language school there for its own missionaries and any others who desired to come. A TEAM missionary rented his summer cabin to us. It needed to be somewhat winterized. About all he could do was to enclose the space under the house with cement blocks which he did. We moved in finding ourselves in an entirely different environment in this mountain village. And very much on our own. The other students and the teachers became family to us. One of our Japanese teachers had a son the same age as our Steven. His name was Joe chan. Living near us was a missionary family from Okinawa. They were with the Far Eastern Broadcasting Company, a missionary radio station. They had two boys the ages of our boys. The five boys entered the local Yochien (kindergarten). Joe chan was Japanese so understood well what the teachers were saying. Our boys, however, could not. So the four gaijin (foreign) boys proceeded to get into whatever mischief they could. It soon became evident that they were giving their teachers a very bad time. Havoc broke loose. So we withdrew all four from the school much to the relief of the staff.

The winters in the mountains were absolutely gorgeous. Our village sat at the foot of a live volcano, Mt. Asama. Everything was covered with snow. Mt. Asama reached into the bright blue sky with white steam shooting out of her crater hundreds of feet into the sky. Our village lay at 5000 feet above sea level and Mt. Asama's summit at 8,000 feet. Just across the dirt road from our house was a rushing stream, it's banks and rocks deep with snow. I took a wooden box and made skis for it. Fastening it behind my motorized bicycle I would pull the boys around much to their delight. In the summer I put another wooden box on the back of the bike for the boys to ride in. It was much fun. We bought them double bladed skates and made a very rough ice pond for them to skate on. Also in our village we had a ski run for the older ones. It was equipped with a rope tow. On that slope I and other students would practice our language skills with other skiers. It was great.

Mount Asama

The only heat we had in our little house was a pot-bellied stove which sat just inside the living room from our "one-fanny" kitchen. Outside the kitchen door sat a fifty gallon barrel of oil. The only way we could get oil to the pot-bellied stove was to pump it out of the barrel into a five-gallon can, carry it into the house and pour it into the tank on the back of the stove. After a few trips in the cold I decided there had to be a better way. In Korea we had used hospital tubing to get oil to our little pot-bellied stove in our tent. Off I went in search of plastic tubing. Obtaining some I returned and managed to affix it to the barrel drum. Now what? The floor in the kitchen had a knot hole about two inches in diameter in the floor. I put the oil barrel up on a high stand, ran the tube from it, under the house and up the knot-hole to the stove. It worked. No more chipping ice from around the barrel and carrying five gallon cans into the house.

Soon another problem arose. The water pipes under the house froze. We had the solution. Among the items we had brought from the States was a heating pad. I wrapped the pad around the pipes and brought the cord through the same knot-hole, plugged it in and voila, no more frozen pipes.

Missionary life most anywhere involves some unique, if ugly, innovation. We had a sunken bath tub in our very little bathroom. It is known as an "ofuro". Next to that we had a washing machine which had a vibrator that went up and down, rather than from side to side. Since the floor was not that solid it tended to move around. One day I heard Marilyn call for help from the bath room. I ran to her aid to find that she was trapped in the corner by the moving washing machine. Being pregnant at the time she was in a pickle to say the least. What to do? I moved the washing machine so she could get out. Then the proverbial light bulb went off. We had an old tire outside which I got and put under the washing machine. Now it could bounce all it wanted and not move. It was not quite what one wanted in one's bathroom, but it worked.

During all our missionary life there were times when our financial support either did not arrive on time or was not enough to last a month. We were learning what it is to live by faith. God always supplied by one means or another. This time it had not arrived and we were nearly out of food and no money to buy more. We managed to have formula for the baby and milk. We were about to experience another of God's supply miracles. Our house sat right next to the road, only a couple of feet from it. Everything was volcanic pumice, rock and pebbles. So the ground shook a lot. Just as we were praying a truck rumbled by shaking the house. We looked out the window to see it pass. To our surprise out of the back of the little truck fell a large squash. It did not shatter on the road, but rolled to the side. I immediately retrieved it and we had dinner of delicious squash that night. That might have been a coincidence had it not happened again exactly the same a few months later.

Every house in the village had a number and a sign with the occupants name on it. Our sign read in English, PONTIUS. One day I noticed that painted under the name in identical letter style was the name PILATE. Puzzled, we asked all of our friends if they had done it. No one would admit to having done it.. That winter I received an unusual phone call from Tokyo. We had just then gotten our house phone. The caller identified himself as a priest from the Roman Catholic Diocese in Tokyo. He told me that they had a retreat on the outskirts of Karuizawa. There were two nuns caring for it who where snowed in and could not get to the woodshed for wood for their heating stove. Would I go and help them. Of course I would. Finding the little house they were wintering in, I had to dig through several feet of snow to open a path to the woodshed and from the house to the road. Afterward the ladies invited me in for tea and some very delicious pastry. While we were talking one of the nuns began to giggle. Finally, she said " "Have you seen your house sign lately?" Then she proceeded to tell me that they had been walking past our place last summer and had seen the name PONTIUS. They couldn't resist coming back one night and painting PILATE by flashlight. Mystery solved. We all had a good laugh, and a nice friendship was born.

"Where's Steven?" I heard Marilyn call. We looked everywhere, went to our fellow missionaries' house, but no Steven. So we began going around the neighborhood. A wealthy Japanese man owned a summer home not far away. There was a maid there taking care of it for him. As we approached and entered the genkan (closed in porch) we saw Steve's little shoes resting on the step. In Japan it is the custom to always take one's shoes off before entering a home. Announcing our presence we soon heard the shoji (paper paneled door) open. The house keeper was smiling and there at the low table sitting on a zabaton cushion was Steven, a cup of tea in his little hand and of course cookies on a plate. She had been delighted when he came "calling" at her door. Everyone loved Steven with his near-white hair. In fact all our boys often got squealing hugs from Japanese grandmas dressed in their kominos. Making our polite goodbyes we returned home with Steve in tow.

As I progressed in language school we were required to have some Christian service assignment. Mine was to accompany the evangelistic team every month some distance to a leprosarium some four hours away. It was a tiring trip around Mt. Asama north through muddy roads. On one trip we got stuck wheels deep in a mud hole. The mother of one of our missionaries was with us. It was a delight to see her take off her shoes and step almost knee deep into the mud to help push us out. Of course the proper photos were taken which probably are in her scrap book to this day. These trips were some of the high lights of our missionary service. Marilyn did not come with us as she was several months pregnant and it was not safe for her. Leprosy is not as contagious as it used to be, but we wanted to take precautions. The leprosarium was located at a hot springs which flowed from the volcano. Huge bamboo pipes carry the sulfur water to the many pools at the hospital. Leprosy is a terrible disease. It infects the body by killing the nerves. Then injuries and infections which can not be felt eat away at the flesh, fingers drop off, eyes drop out and toes and feet are destroyed. There was a small group of about twenty believers there. One outstanding man was lying in a hospital bed. His nose had been eaten away and his eyes gone. We fellowshipped at length with him. Our last song was "Itsukushi mi fukaki - What a Friend We Have in Jesus". Over and over he would ask us to sing it again. With tears flowing down my face, we sang as I held his bandaged had which had to be changed every hour due to the body fluids soaking it. I could not imagine the pain he was in, yet he worshipped the Lord with enthusiasm.

My Japanese teacher asked me, "George, do you remember Isaiah 9:6 says that our sins are as filthy rags? The word for filthy rags really means leper's rags. Before me was a living illustration of that verse.

It was at this leprosarium I gave my first testimony in Japanese over the intercom of the hospital. It was terrible. I asked a patient if he understood. Jokingly he replied that he did not as he could not understand English. I don't really know if anyone really did understand. Perhaps the Lord gave a miracle of hearing to their ears. Among the lepers was a stately Russian woman and her son. They were members of the Czar's family who had fled Russia at the revolution. They were devout believers and a joy to visit. In Karuizawa there were also two Russian ladies of royal descent. I loved visiting them as they had the best Russian pastries. Many years later as I ate the same kind of pastries in Siberia I was reminded once again of these dear believers. They are all in glory now. Someday we will be reunited with them again.

CLIMB THE MOUNTAIN

"Why do you want to climb an active volcano?", Marilyn asked me. "Because it's there," I jokingly replied. We were in charge of the youth group during Japan Evangelical Missionary Association's annual summer conference held at the large JEMA church in Kariuzawa. Several teenagers, some Japanese, some missionary kids asked me to lead the climb. The trail was very steep and traversed back and forth up the mountain. It was best to begin in the early evening in order to be at the rim by sunrise. Though it was a summer night it would be very cold at the top of the mountain so we dressed warmly. We had flashlights, drink and food in our packs. Along the way were several make-shift shrines with food and drink offerings for those who had committed suicide by jumping into the volcano. Many volcanoes in Japan are nicked named *"suicide mountain"*. At about the 7,000 foot level we passed through a thick cloud layer almost obliterating the trail. Now as the elevation got higher we had to sit down to rest more frequently. Exiting the clouds the sky was clear and we could see the red glow of the lava pit above us. The rim of the crater was narrow. The inside of the crater slanted down for about fifteen feet and then plunged straight down 600 feet to the lava below. There was no dome, just boiling and spitting hot lava. The stench of sulfur caused us to hug the ground under the layer of steam that flowed over the ledge about three feet above the ground. It was about sunrise when we stood up, our upper bodies above the sulfur cloud. As more light begin to creep up we noticed that Kariuzawa and everything below was covered with clouds. The only thing we could see was Mt. Fuji rising out of the clouds to our south west. Then it happened. A bright yellow orb seemed to rise right out of Mt. Fuji. It was sunrise. We just stood there. No one spoke. We were a few guys standing alone above the clouds, the only ones on earth it seemed. The beauty of God's creation filled our hearts and souls. Slowly we all uttered "Wow". I turned to the group of young people. "And this Creator loves us and died for us," I whispered. I don't think there was a dry eye in the group.

As we descended the mountain, weary from no sleep, we found fields of Asama berries. These were the huckleberries we knew at home. Stopping and stuffing our stomachs with berries. We also filled every container and our backpacks with Asama berries thinking of hot berry pie when we got home.

Mean time "back at the ranch," Marilyn was anxious as we were hours late returning. It turned out that just an hour or so after we started our climb the TV announced that the mountain was closed due to an expected eruption. We did arrive home safely on that trip. On another trip up the mountain we took rechargeable flashlights that were supposed to run twenty hours. They quit after only three hours. We lost the trail and started around the mountain on the opposite side. It was extremely cold, cloudy and damp Suddenly I had a dreadful feeling. I told everyone to stop right where they were, come to me and sit down. We huddled together for warmth and waited for dawn. When it came the clouds lifted a little. I was startled to see that we had rounded the mountain on the other side. Within a few feet in front of us was a one thousand foot cliff left from an ancient eruption. Had we kept going we stood a good chance of falling over that cliff. Some may doubt the existence of guardian angels. I don't.

PLEASE NOT NOW, LORD

We had just purchased a California style stucco house outside of Tachikawa Air Force Base. The US Air force was preparing to return the base to the Japanese so these houses were for sale. It was a gift from God. We borrowed the $5000 from my parents and were preparing to move in. We were renting the land on which the house sat for $11 a year with a ninety nine year lease. By then we had moved from the little village house to another missionary's house which sat on the side of a large hill just outside of town. While living there the large Nagano earthquake took place just fifty miles to the west of us on the eastern Japanese seacoast. I was outside and Marilyn was inside. Suddenly the hill behind our house began to literally roll like waves coming ashore. It hit the house knocking many things down and splitting the porch. Both of us were knocked down. Because this house had foundations that ran under every room, there was virtually no damage. Soon many helicopters flew overhead toward Nagano. Later that week our missionaries gathered food and supplies and headed for the city. It had flooded, huge oil storage tanks had exploded. The ground had opened up swallowing a little girl up to her waist. Apartment buildings lay on their sides exposing only four feet of foundation. The builder was arrested later for violating building codes. Everything seemed desolate. However, standing alone among many shattered houses stood the Christian Church. It seemed a beacon of God in a devastated city. It was being used for rescue work .

I had been busy every summer while in language school with Bible camps. One of my best friends, a TEAM missionary, and I ran English Bible camps for Japanese and another TEAM friend ran Joy Bible Camp for missionary and other foreign kids. These were a great joy. At one camp I decided with another missionary friend to go scuba diving off the swimming beach below the camp. We had been scouring the bottom at about fifty feet when I began to gasp for air. Rising only ten feet more air was released from my scuba tanks. Soon however the air was gone. I looked below for my diving partner. Not seeing him I headed for the surface. I immediately saw that the swells had risen significantly. I put my snorkel in my mouth and gulped a mouthful of sea water. I thought I was going to drown. I undid my weight belt and let it drop and was about to ditch my air tank when I felt my diving partner nudge me up above the surface. I freed my kinked snorkel tube and began gasping air. We were about fifty yards from shore.

We had also drifted away from the small beach. In front of us were high rock cliffs on top of which rested the camp. Waves were crashing onto the cliffs and shore. Finding a small ledge we decided we would let the waves carry us up and toss us onto it. To our left a rock spur ran down to the beach. We hugged the cliff on the narrow ledge and inched our way to the spur. However, it was separated from the ledge by about four feet. My dive buddy was able to jump the four feet with the waves twenty feet below. He urged me to jump also. But my knees were like rubber and I could do nothing but hug the cliff. Climbing down the ledge he called for help. No answer. He returned to my place on the ledge. By now I had quit shaking and was able to jump to the spur and get down to the beach. Totally exhausted we lay on the beach. After much yelling help arrived from the camp above. Dinner was already underway. I was to be the evening speaker that day and everyone was wondering where we were.

Returning to Karuizawa we purchased groceries and were climbing the fifty steps up to the house when I heard and felt something rip in my abdomen. I had previously been plagued with hernias, having had two surgeries. I knew right away what had happened. I called the Essai Biyoin, a Seventh Day Adventist hospital that served the Japanese as well as the missionary community. The doctor told me to get down right away and he would schedule surgery. We packed up a few things for a few days' stay, called our fellow missionaries at New Life League compound and headed down the two hundred fifty hairpin turns off the mountain. The next day I underwent surgery. It was a success and within a few days we returned to Karuizawa.

That was only the beginning, During surgery a contaminated incision became infected with hospital staph we now know as MRSA. I had a boil at the incision site the size of a baseball. It was extremely painful. Another call to the hospital and another quick drive down the mountain. We had an old car which had a large hole in the floor in front of the back seat, over which a plywood board had been placed. There were no seat belts in those days for our two boys who rode in the back seat. Marilyn held the baby in her arms and prayed that no one would fall through that hole. Arriving at the house of our fellow missionaries, Roy and Doris, I jumped into Roy's car and we headed for the hospital. Immediately upon examination the doctor tried to lance the boil by shoving a large needle into the center of it thinking that the area was still anesthetized from the surgery. It wasn't. Roy was by then out in the parking lot getting ready to leave when he heard my scream. Picking up the phone the doctor immediately ordered the operation room readied. The doctor removed several ounces of infection and sewed me up again. That was on a Friday. I was released and told to return on Monday. On Monday he took one look at me and ordered surgery again. This time he kept me in the hospital. The MRSA had spread everywhere. I was covered with boils on my torso, face and limbs. Slowly I slipped into a coma and was placed in isolation. Marilyn overheard the doctors talking about my not surviving and that they should tell Marilyn to prepare to return home.

By that time we had moved into our newly purchased house in Nakagami Machi and the phone had been installed. Marilyn promised the Lord that she would remain and do what missionary work she could if I died. Early one morning the phone rang. It was the doctor. He had woken up and thought of an idea. He would make a cocktail of antibiotics and see if that worked. It did and I was responding. That spring we returned for our first furlough. We booked passage on a Japanese cruise ship, the Brazil Maru. At a shower before we left Spokane we had been given a large bag of safety razors. We now knew the reason why. I could not use a razor a second time so needed all those razors to shave while I was recovering. Marilyn was taught how to lance the boils. She would do so while I yelled in pain. We took a picture of the family on the Brazil Maru. I look like I had lost twenty pounds, which I had and my face was thin and scarred from the boils. God had, however rescued me from death and we would return for another term in Japan

CHAPTER SIX

THE MOUNTAINS SHALL SING

THE DOG

The several missionary families that had left New Life League and entered into evangelism ministry soon found that they needed some structure and accountability to one another. We met together along with two other families that were soon to join us to discus the formation of a governing mission. The mistakes of the past that we had experienced ourselves and had seen in other organizations were something we labored to avoid. The name of the new mission was by unanimous decision *Japan Rural Evangelism Fellowship (J.R.EF)*. A home board was selected. However, they would have only advisory authority. Decisions would be made on the field by the missionaries present. Since we were a small mission we chose a Congregational form of government with everyone sharing the vote. To maintain harmony we followed 1 Timothy 5:19 "Do not entertain an accusation against an elder unless it is brought by two or three witnesses. (NIV)". Thus we became accountable to one another in love, discipline, encouragement, support and work.

Since we were traveling evangelists and were dedicated to reaching rural areas we would gather together each month for prayer and planning. We held evangelist crusades in small towns and villages. At this time we would share ideas about where next to hold a series of meetings. A map was laid on the table and we would peruse it, pray and together choose the area or town by unanimous agreement.

The Central Japan Pioneer Mission Australia and New Zealand had worked for many years in establishing indigenous churches throughout central Japan. When they had some forty churches and one seminary they turned the work over to the local churches. The denomination formed was the *Fukuin Dendo Kyodan (Gospel Evangelical Church)*. Since there were no missionaries left with them they were in need of help. So it was that we entered into ministry of Gospel Crusades sponsored by the local churches. These were to be held in English with interpretation to draw youth wanting to be exposed to English speaking people. The week of the crusade we would travel to the church. There on Wednesday and Thursday we would hold meetings for the believers and evangelistic services on the weekend. We advertised with large posters around town, radio announcement fliers, and *Denwa Hoso*. Each telephone had a loud speaker in it. Announcements were made over the phone usually from the town or city officials. However, we could purchase time cheaply and every phone announced the crusade, thus *Denwa Hoso (telephone advertising)*.

Another means of getting the word out was corner evangelism. A couple of us would take our *senden (loud speaker)* car to an area. We would drive around with the speakers on top advertising the meetings. Then we would choose a corner. Frank and I would set up a microphone. He would play the guitar and we would sing Christian hymns, give a short explanation of the Gospel, an invitation to the evening meeting and we were gone. On one such occasion there was no one around. We decided to do our corner thing anyway. No sooner had we begun when a dog strolled up and sat down in front of us. Apparently he liked to sing also as he began to accompany us with a loud howl. Frank and I looked at each other and could not hold back a laugh. We quickly packed up the car and left. That evening many came to the service. Among them was a young man about twenty three years old. To our joy he responded to the invitation to receive Christ as

His personal Savior. During the counseling session that followed we asked him what brought him to the crusade. It was our purpose to evaluate the different methods we had used to advertise the meetings. His reply astonished us. "It was the dog," he said. Further explaining, he said he had been in an upstairs room just above us when he heard us sing. Then the dog came. "I thought", he said, "if these foreigners can embarrass themselves like that the least I can do is go hear what they had to say." It ceases to amaze me the lengths the Holy Spirit uses to draw someone to Himself.

CRUSADES AND PRISON MINISTRY

Our mission work took us to very small mountain villages and some quite large rural towns. In between crusades we engaged in door-to-door evangelism. We often followed a river high into the mountains. Finding the farthest village and climbing many hills led us to thatched roofed houses high on a mountain slope with stair-stepped rice paddies. Moving down the river we took each tributary valley and began at it's top working our way down the valley. This took us nearly ten years. It had been a long day and the last hill lay before us. Both of us were tired. We flipped a coin. I lost, or won, the toss and went up the steep path to a little house at the top. Sitting on the wooden porch was a little old lady, probably in her nineties. When she saw me coming up the path she got up. Surprised to see a foreigner she smiled. Soon she brought out a pot of tea and some *osembe (rice crackers)*. As I eventually began to tell the Gospel story she began to sing -*"Shu wa Iesu, ai su."* Her voice was soft and sweet. Immediately I joined her in song. "Jesus Loves Me" seems the same in any language. How did she know it? Her story unfolded. As a small girl she lived in a village where a missionary lived. It was in his Sunday School she learned that Jesus loved her. She had not seen a missionary again, but listened faithfully to Christian radio. What a privilege to share with another of God's loved ones.

Prisons in Japan are bleak and cold. A fellow missionary from TEAM, Russell, worked with our evangelistic team. His ministry was in Christian films. The complete story of Christ was on several reels. On top of his American station wagon he had installed a flat platform on which was mounted a projector and movie screen. We would find an open field or area, park the car and show the movie. The audience would sit in front of the car viewing the movie projected from behind the screen. There was always a crowd. Afterward the Gospel was explained, counseling given and new believers were assigned to one of the churches for follow up. Because of the movies Russell and our team had been given free access to all Japanese prisons. Showings were held in the dining halls and converts were enrolled in a radio Bible correspondence course for follow up. Though there were some Americans in the prisons we never had contact with any of them. Often traveling between the prisons took some time.

The monthly JREF prayer and planning gatherings went well. One crusade was most memorable. We chose a fairly large town to the south of Tokyo. All the usual preparations were made. However on the first night of the crusade no one came. This had never happened before. Many of us missionaries taught English at Tokyo language schools. The next night Tom brought with him two students, one guy and his girlfriend. A regular preaching session was not held. However the movie was shown. Afterward we sat down with the couple and in conversation explained the Gospel. Their response was that Christianity was for women and children. No one else came.

After we had returned from our third furlough we learned eight months later that we would have to return to the States permanently because of the fact all our boys had scoliosis and proper treatment was not available in Japan. Shortly after that there was a knock at our door. It was Kazunori-san, the student from our "failed" crusade. In ignorance Tom, who had brought Kazunori-san to the meeting, was sent home by his sponsoring church saying that because no one was converted at that meeting God had told them that Tom was not a missionary. It broke Tom's heart.

"Are you going home?" was Kazunori's question at the door. We ushered him in. Marilyn served the customary tea and crackers. "Do you remember the meeting where I and my friend were the only ones?" "Of course," I replied. He went on to explain that on the train home he was deep in thought. The wheels of the train seemed to say to him - "you're a sinner...you're a sinner" with every clack of the wheels. It was a few weeks before he decided to get in touch with us. However, we had left for our second furlough. He came looking for our fellow missionaries. Soon he became a solid believer and was now studying in Bible school.

Suddenly Kazunori-san said, "I'm your replacement." The look on my face must have been surprising. He went on to tell me that the Lord had been urging him to take up the rural ministry we had after we left. Wow! God does supply even someone to help continue the ministry. Later we were to learn that he had married and they had a little girl they named Mary after Marilyn.

But I am getting ahead of my story.

CHAPLAINS AND DOLLS

During our second term one afternoon our boys called us to look out of the window. In front was a U.S. Marine staff car and a big six-by truck. Opening the door I was astonished to see my chaplain from Korea. We both hugged each other, military proto-call set aside. We spent some time recalling our days with the 5th Regiment, 1st Marine Division. It was really great to see him again. He was the chaplain who had baptized me in the Imjim river on the 38th parallel in Korea. It was the renewing of a great friendship. He was then the Chaplain at Kamisea Naval Air Base in central Japan not far from us. "I've got something for you if you can use them." With that he led me to the truck outside which took up the entire width of our narrow street. Opening the back he showed me dozens of Chatty Kathy dolls. "Do you know of children that would like these?" he asked. I certainly did as we had connection with a children's hospital. The marines brought them all in and lined them up on every couch and chair we had. It was afternoon and our youngest was in bed. We heard Jerry shout "Babies." He had just awakened from his nap and entered the living room.

How the chaplain found us I do not know except we did receive a letter one time addressed only as to George Pontius, Japan. The Japanese immigration service did keep close watch on all foreigners. Later I was Auxillary Chaplain for him at Kamisea Naval Air Station chapel while he was gone. It was through this that I met soldiers from Zama Army Hospital. This was the main hospital that received wounded from Vietnam. They had begun an evening evangelistic service in the base chapel. I soon became their pastor. Shortly the church, now called Zama Baptist Church, moved off base to a kindergarten which they rented on Sundays. I became the morning pastor and one of my best friends from Joy Bible Camp became the evening pastor. One Sunday evening on his way to Zama his car broke down on the freeway. One of the church members came for him. Upon his return that night he noticed that his car had not yet been towed. They stopped so he could retrieve something he needed from his car. The freeway at this point was 80 feet above ground. Not realizing that the opposite lanes were not connected he jumped over the railing and fell eighty feet landing in a muddy creek bed below. Dozens of bones were broken including his legs in numerous places. However, he was conscious. To get to him one had to go to the next off ramp and travel back along the bridge to find him. An ambulance was called. It was pitch black under the bridge. My friend had a wonderful tenor voice which he often contributed to our crusades. So he began to sing. It was the beacon needed to find him. Because he was with an army soldier when he fell they took him to the Zama Army hospital.

Ever since the church had been asked to leave the base we had been praying for a Gospel presence to minister there. There were many surgeries. After each Jim was in terrific pain. To relieve his stress he sang. His private room was near the ward where many wounded were being treated. He was asked to be rolled into the hallway or ward so they could hear his singing. Through his wonderful voice and counseling the Gospel permeated the hospital. God had answered our prayers for the hospital, but a terrible price had been paid.

After many months TEAM decided that Jim should return to the States for rehabilitation. By now his medical bills had sky-rocketed. Another reason to pray. A fund was set up for that purpose. Soldiers, Missionaries and Japanese believers gave generously. It was not nearly enough as he needed room for his stretcher on a commercial plane at great cost. Just before his schedule departure the base comptroller asked him for his permission to write about his case in the Army Journal of Medicine in return for which his entire hospital and surgical bills would be waived. The money he had in his fund was enough to pay for the plane fare for him and his entire family. I saw him many years later, very scarred but serving the Lord as a pastor in the Seattle area.

Zama Baptist Church was erecting its own building in conjunction with the Japanese Baptist Convention. When the military left, the Japanese congregation would be given the church. The dedication of the new church was held the day we had to leave Japan so I never got to preach from that pulpit. How satisfying to know that it was completed and dedicated.

It was near Christmas. Marilyn and I did our shopping once a month in Tokyo at a small Intermission Grocery Market in Tokyo that stocked American food. It was one of those times that our money was low and the giving was low. We went to the store, a three hour drive, with all non-essential items crossed off our list. This meant no Christmas tree, only little gifts for the boys and no candy or Christmas extras. We were well seasoned in knowing that the Lord promises to supply all our needs, not necessarily our wants. We bought all our necessities and were thankful for His gifts to us.

Later that evening we were home with the groceries on the dining room table along with the original crossed-off list. About seven or eight that evening we received a phone call from an Air Force pilot on the near by Yokota Air Base saying that they wanted to visit us. Of course we agreed. For the life of me I could not remember who he was. His name did seem vaguely familiar. They arrived shortly thereafter. We did not even have coffee to serve them as it was not one of the necessary items on our list. When I got up my nerve I ask them why they had come as I did not remember him. He reminded me that I would receive radio broadcast tapes from Far Eastern Broadcasting Company in Okinawa and deliver them to our local Christian station. He was one of the pilots that ferried them from Kadena Air Base on Okinawa to Yokota Air base near us. Then I remembered. Still I was curious why he had come. He explained further that every year he and his wife prayed about a missionary family they could provide Christmas for. This year it was ours. With that said they went to their car and brought in sack after sack of groceries, toys and gifts. There was a small Christmas tree also. These were items we could not get as we did not have access to the base commissary. Soon they departed with our many thanks.

No sooner had their car disappeared down the street than we sent Steven to retrieve our mutilated grocery list. Typical of the Lord's abundance, every item we had crossed off was in those sacks. In addition great toys for the boys and us, Christmas candy and everything we could desire.

There were other times when money was low and we found that Intermissions had special sales on many things we needed. Experiences of God's grace was not confined to us. Our dear friends and fellow missionaries, Frank and Noeline, had a wealthy visitor from New Zealand. Upon departure he told them that if they ever needed anything just let him know and he would supply it. However, Frank was not comfortable fearing he might ask for something not in the Lord's will. "I will tell the Lord our needs, and if you hear the Lord's whisper you can respond." Many weeks later Noeline and Frank were down to their last penny. While discussing this the postmen came to the door and handed them a registered letter. In it was a large check and the words "I heard the Lord's whisper"

THE TELEGRAM

The routine of our crusades and door to door ministry settled in to be broken only by summer camp ministry.

This ministry often took me away from home for days and weeks at a time. Marilyn was left to be mother and father to the boys. Our three oldest attended the Christian Academy in Japan at Kurume. We had a bus for some time but when that was no longer available the boys had to ride three trains making two changes to get to school. Jerry was the smallest, being first grade. The older boys would board the train and immediately face the side with little Jerry in front of them. They would then place their arms on the wall to protect him from the morning rush hour crush. One day we were to pick up the boys after school. Tim and Steve argued. Steve rightly saying that we were coming to the school. Tim , on the other hand thought we were to meet them at the train station near home. Tim left to return by train. When we got to the school Steve told us what happened. We called Frank and asked him to meet the train and take Tim home with him until we got there. Some time later before we had left the Academy we got a phone message that Tim did not get off the train. Frightened we cancelled our dinner date with friends. Arriving home to find Tim at Frank's we learned that he had fallen asleep and woke up in the mountains. With the help of a train conductor he got on the return train and finally to the right station. It was frightening as the boys did not speak or understand much Japanese.

There were Air Force and other American personnel living in our neighborhood. Frequently the neighbor ladies would gather for coffee and conversation like ladies do. Our next door lady was one who came over almost every day to visit with Marilyn. She was a confused lady who was going through her third divorce.

One day a telegram arrived informing me of my father's death. Immediately I sent home word that I could not be there for the funeral and would my brother assure my step-mother of my love and sympathy. The telegram lay on the coffee table. The next day, having shed some tears, I left with the team to do our usual mission work. That morning our neighbor arrived as usual. As Marilyn was bringing coffee there was a gasp from the living room. Our neighbor had read the telegram. "Where is George?" she inquired. Marilyn mentioned that I had gone to work as usual. "How could he, isn't he devastated by his father's death?" It was an opportunity of a life time. Marilyn gently shared the hope we have in Christ, the love of God clearly to her. "I see you really believe and live what you say," was her answer. However, she believed that her "suffering" would earn her a place in heaven and days out of purgatory. With sadness we realized that she was not receiving the Word of God about grace vs. works. Later I would meet with her and her fourth husband in the cafeteria of Harvard University where he was a professor. They never understood that it is by grace through faith that one believes, not works.

I HATE GOD

"Mommy, where's Daddy?," a little voice inquired. "He's out doing God's work," the mother replied. "I hate God," the little boy said. Taken back by his bold statement Marilyn said nothing. Silence filled the room like a cold mist. Gathering her thoughts she asked, "Why do you hate God?" "Because He's always taking my Daddy away." As we talked about this incident later we both realized that our priorities were somewhat askew. It was often taught that God came first, then the ministry and lastly the family. Many a pastor and missionary have lost their children by this false teaching. The truth is that our priority should be God first, family second and ministry last. That is why Paul taught that it is better for a man in the Lord's work not to be married and thus burdened with other responsibilities. He is not saying that one should not be married, but that we must recognize the importance of the family.

We were slow to learn that lesson. It is most difficult to do so when churches demand so much of their pastors and missionaries, demands they would never put upon themselves. We were later to learn the truth of that the hard way.

One of our missionaries, Roy, had some property along the beach at a place a place called Toji. Often the mission families would go there for a time of rest. A hostel would be built with the help of our Zama Baptist friends and a camp held for college students. This beach was a remote beach accessible by car only through a man-made tunnel hewn out of solid rock. We called this camp, Izu, according to the peninsula it was on. There were caves along the shore to explore. A flat rock at the ocean end of a large hill was a great fishing place. To get there we had to creep along a very narrow ledge around the side with the ocean many feet below. Scuba diving was great. There was a nearby beach we called Agate Beach for the agates we could find. It was completely enclosed except of a narrow passage through the rocks to the ocean. That passage was about fifty feet deep. We could swim through with our scuba gear but had to watch for huge moray eels lurking in every cleft. On the beach where the cabin was far from shore was a small shipwrecked vessel. With every wave it would capsize always to right itself. The protected surf on that beach was florescent and glowed beautifully in the night. The entire family would sit on a tall picnic table I had made and watch the shining waves and the sparkling stars.

The road down to the beach was full of clay. When wet there was no returning up the road. We were at Toji one summer when a typhoon was suddenly upon us. There was no electricity so we had no radio to hear weather reports. I had built the boys a toy airplane of large plywood on the ground. During that storm it really did take flight as did Jerry's underwear which Tim threw into the air. The wind was horrific as we huddled in the hostel. Afterward the road was slick clay. We were stranded for several days. Hiking to the little village of Toji we were able to keep supplied with food. It truly is a happy family memory.

One day we crawled around the big rocky hill on the little ledge to the flat fishing area. There was a blow hole there that sent great spouts of water into the air with every big wave. That day fisherman had hooked a grouper which is a large wide-mouthed fish about 300 lbs. It took them all night to land that fish. Groupers were friendly to scuba divers, though somewhat frightening. Some would feed them with fish they had speared.

The nearest town to Toji was Shimoda. There the first Americans landed to visit the Emperor. It was on Shimoda beach that the famous movie, *Shogun*, was filmed. We had done door-to-door evangelism on that very beach. Watching the film we could see the very houses we had visited. Shimoda also has a nice outdoor aquarium where one can swim with dolphins. The boys and I took a small rowboat into the lagoon. Soon dolphins were jumping over our boat much to the delight of the boys.

I was Scout Leader on Tachikawa base for the Webelos. We did lots of things scouts do. Then that summer the World Scout Jamboree was held in Japan. The Japanese committee chose the windward side of Mt. Fuji for the huge world encampment. They were told that it was not wise to camp there during typhoon season. But the camp was built anyway. A typhoon slammed directly into the mountain camp area causing heavy flooding and devastation. Only the Japanese and American contingents remained. The Japanese Scout Committee took refuge in an old WWII bunker on the mountain. The US Forces rescued the others. A day or so later the typhoon was gone and the scouts returned. It was then that Marilyn and I took the Webelos to the jamboree. Most of the tents were erected again. As the scouts visited each other's camp sites much trading took place; patches, hats and anything they could get. Of course the Scottish scouts were asked to trade their kilts but not one would part with them. Steve and Tim were some of the smallest scouts there. They were really cute in their uniforms. Often mamma-sans would touch their white hair or want to hug them. This was difficult for Steve who was quite shy. I lost count of how many photos were taken of the boys with Japanese families. It was the scouting experience of a life time.

THE FRUIT OF THE WORD

Back in language school I had joined with TEAM missionaries to minister in Joy Bible Camp and English Bible Camps for Japanese students. Joy Bible Camp was great. The kids loved being with "Uncle" Lyle, "Aunt" June, "Uncle" George and others. Lots of stories, lessons, songs and play were the order of the day.

The English Bible Camps were for Japanese high school and college students. English was the calling card. All lessons were interpreted except the evening Gospel meeting which was taught by a local pastor. Marilyn and the boys would on occasion join us in these camps. One evening shortly after the vesper service we missionaries who had been in another room praying while the pastor shared the Gospel, heard soft footsteps on the wooden floor. "Gomen Kudasai," she said softly at the shoji door. "Ohairi kudasai" we replied. Slowly the high school girl opened the sliding paper door and entered. She was dressed in a lovely kimono. "I just became your sister," she announced. We were surprised at the interesting way she told us that she had become a Christian. Apparently she understood the family of God.

After another such camp one of the campers, Hiromichi, wrote; "Dear My Teacher, I am very sorry to have not sent you any letters, please forgive me. After that camp, I could have chance to take the examination… Bye the bye I am to be baptized the 20th of this month, December, from Mr. Chase and Mr. Ikeda. How happy I am! I wish everybody in the world could know how wonderful, nice, splendid …(though words are too few for me to say or express) to be done so if they are qualified…I can't stop thinking for my Savior Jesus Christ. Also I will not be able to forget the experience of summer time which I could have at Tateyama forever.

Good bye
Hiromichi

CHAPTER SEVEN

REUNION AND REPORTS

HOMEWARD BOUND

How quickly time goes by. Four years passed since we sat foot on Japanese soil and Mailyn had squeezed my hand and said, "We're home." Four years of learning, ministering, seeing the Lord's miraculous supply and His healing. We had set our first term for five years. However, since the previous fall when I was at death's door I was still fighting many boils and was thus in a weakened condition, we decided to take our furlough a year early. My health was slowly returning. The more than twenty pounds I had lost was not yet half regained. My face was drawn and pocked with scars and remaining boils. In fact it was on the ship home that the final boil was incised by the ship's doctor. We really needed the rest of a furlough.

It was absolutely necessary for me to rest before beginning the rigorous task of deputation.

Furloughs for missionaries are filled with mixed emotions. On the one hand it was a joy to think of seeing family and old friends. However, on the other hand, we would leave behind, though temporarily, so many new friends, including students and converts. Indeed we were becoming "Japanese" in our adopted land. There were many good byes before we boarded the ship. At the dock were numerous friends. We did not realize how many. The faces of our young students, converts, missionary friends looked up at us as we stood at the railing. Marilyn had broken a toe leaving for the dock and was in pain. Our hearts were also in pain. Rolls of ticker tape were thrown to us from the dock. Our friends held onto one end and we the other. As the tug nudged our ship away from the dock the tape would stretch as we let the rolls peel out. Finally we came to the end of the roll. The ship moved slowly out to sea. The tape stretched and stretched and finally broke. Tears welled up. When we could no longer see the dock we slipped below to our cabins and wept a bit, then settled in for the long journey home. We learned later that the many friends on the dock stayed there holding their end of the tape until the smoke from our ships stacks disappeared on the horizon.

We had two state rooms, one for us and one for our three boys. The boys had the outer cabin where they could sit in a porthole and watch the see appear and disappear as the small ship rolled in the waves. The boys soon learned that we had our own personal steward. They were delighted to order snacks and breakfast in bed. The dining room was just across the passage way from our cabins. Meals were served in five courses starting with fish, soup, vegetables, entrée and dessert. Having been the Navy I did not get sea sick. However, Marilyn and the boys felt queasy even having taken sea sick pills.

The Brazil Maru was a small passenger ship, so the facilities such as the swimming pool were small. Water would slop over the sides of the pool as the ship rolled in the billows. On board was the Japanese Olympic swimming team. They soon took our two older boys under their wing and we hardly saw them the whole trip except for dinner. However, there was a knock at our stateroom one day. Standing outside was one of the ship's sailors with the two boys in hand. It seemed they had gone exploring and ended up in the engine room which was off limits to passengers. A high light for them was getting to be on the bridge and the captain letting them "steer" the ship for a while.

The voyage to Los Angeles was more then two weeks with one stop in Honolulu, Hawaii. As we anchored off Honolulu before dawn we could smell the hibiscus and other flowers. It was much more pleasant than the smell of fish in Tokyo bay or the smell of oil at San Pedro, California. We spent a lovely afternoon going to the Kodak show at Waikiki and visiting other sights around Honolulu. That afternoon we set sail for Los Angeles. A young couple with a couple of kids dilly-dallied in the dock shops and missed the boat. As we began to round Diamond Head we came to a dead stop in the water. Gathering at the rail we watched as this couple caught up to us in a tug. They had to board through a hatch in the lower deck. I imagine that it was an expensive lesson to learn.

Another missionary couple and their two girls were aboard. They were from Sweden and did not speak Japanese. It was a pleasure to the Japanese aboard to listen to the four children communicate in Japanese their only common language. Also aboard was an American couple with children and about forty or so young Japanese Christian ladies going to Brazil for arranged marriages to Japanese missionaries who were serving in Brazil. We were asked to hold a Bible study and worship services by our fellow believers. I approached the Purser who said that we could not because they had a large number of Sokka Gakkai Buddhists aboard with several priests and they would object. This sect was very militant trying to force their beliefs on the Japanese and the whole world if they could. I appealed to the Captain reminding him that the Japanese Constitution guaranteed religious freedom for all. He agreed but told us that if he himself made the arrangements there well might be a riot. However he mentioned that there was a bulletin board in the lounge and if we wanted to advertise a Bible study or worship service, he would not see it. Once begun he would not stop it. That we did. Soon we had a daily Bible study with most all the Christians attending. There were so many of us that the Buddhist priests could not object. On Sundays we held worship services with over fifty passengers in attendance. We used the dining room which was offered to us. However the Sokka Gakkai priests found another way to harass us. Directly above our state room was the dance floor and band stand. These priests set up a big drum and gong which they beat all night. We could not sleep for a couple of nights, but then fell asleep in spite of the noise. About the fourth night other passengers complained and it stopped.

In our Bible study everyone agreed to witness openly for the Lord seeking to win some to Him. The Japanese ladies were going on from Los Angeles to Brazil and the agreed together to continue with the Bible Study and worship services after we left the ship in Los Angeles. By the time we reached California we were having nearly one hundred attending the services.

When the ship docked at the pier in San Pedro south of Los Angeles we went top side and noticed many of our friends from Central Bible Church there to greet us. They had a sign in Japanese characters that read - Welcome Home. Among the smiling faces was Fred, known to our boys as "Fwed." I kept motioning to them as best I could that they were holding the sign upside down. The fellow Japanese passengers were laughing as the sign was turned over. Those waiting to take us to their home had to wait nearly four hours. Somehow customs failed to have an interpreter available for the arrival of a Japanese flag passenger ship. On the dock where everyone was going through customs there was turmoil. Inspector and passenger could not understand each other. I offered to be the interpreter. Thus there was a four hour wait while I helped the customs officials After the last Japanese passenger was finished the official was about to say good bye when I told him we had not yet been through customs. Handing him a list of cameras and equipment I had purchased for friends which would cost several hundred dollars in custom fees I presented the boxes to him. He handed the list back to me and stamped everything as passed with no fees. "Hope that compensates you for your time," he said shaking my hand. God's grace was demonstrated once again.

After our things were loaded into a couple cars we headed for Costa Mesa/Newport Beach to start our furlough. Along the way, Evelyn, one of our dear friends from Costa Mesa, wanted to know if our three boys wanted a Twinkie. "What's a Twinkie", they asked. She replied in surprise, "Poor boys, they do not know what a Twinkie is." Marilyn and I were polite enough not to laugh. We did not consider our boys deprived at all. How many boys had the privilege of living in a colorful land or spending two weeks on a luxury liner? After all Japan was not deepest Africa.

We settled in at Evelyn and Hal's lovely home. The visiting seemed to last well into the night. Tomorrow would begin another phase of our lives, furlough. Little did we know then how exhausting that would be or that we would have to return to Japan to get any rest.

FURLOUGHS ARE NOT REST

We had no more than driven through the dock gates when we were informed that a meeting had been scheduled for that evening. So much for rest. Marilyn was told that the ladies wanted her to speak to them about *her* ministry, not mine. We had long before made the decision that family came before ministry, so Marilyn told them that her ministry was with our children. Therefore we chose not to put them in boarding school, but raise them in the home. The Lord had honored that decision by giving us a house within traveling distance of the Christian Academy. As Marilyn explained her ministry was wife, mother and home maker the look on the lady's face was one of disapproval. She wanted to hear from a *real* missionary for the evening. The ladies meeting did not go well. It is strange the concepts some people have formed about how missionaries should live. Demands on my time and on many a pastors' time are unreasonable. The Pastor is to lead and train the flock. It is the responsibility of the sheep to reproduce. Few church members believe that. That's one reason churches die.

After spending some time in Costa Mesa and the Los Angeles area sharing the grace of the Lord upon our first term on the field we headed home to Spokane. Our supporters were in churches spread all over America. We had purchased a car from Marilyn's father in Los Angeles. Now we faced the task of getting it packed with what we needed for our travel from church to church. Included was an old Arabian canvas tent. It was very heavy. We managed to get everything in its place in the trunk including the tent. The back seat of the small Buick was filled with things up to the seat. Blankets were spread and the boys had the entire back seat area to themselves. There were no seat belts in those days for safety. In addition to all our camping stuff we had pamphlets about the ministry, slides and a projector. We also carried with us an 8mm projector and tape recorder for sound. We were ready for many deputation meetings.

The boys were really excited about the trip all the way to Boston, Mass. and back through the central United States. It would take six weeks of camping out, staying with friends and in an occasional motel. Going east along highway two our first stop was at Glacier National Park. It was a great place to camp with all its beauty. We drove over Going-to-the-Sun highway to the summit. The view was breathtaking. Snow drifts still lined the parking lot. It was a great place for sliding which the boys did. Jerry lost a shoe in the snow which he never found. In another spot in Minnesota we were besieged by mosquitoes as big as birds it seemed. Other campers let Marilyn and the boys stay inside their netted patio while I put up our tent. I think I lost a pint of blood to mosquitoes before I finished. The first thing in the morning we packed up and were out of there. Camped along side a lovely lake in another state a storm suddenly came up and flattened our tent around us. We crossed into Canada at Su St Marie. Then we drove along the Canadian border until we reached Niagara Falls. There we stayed the night before continuing to Boston.

At Boston we stayed with my former Commanding Officer in Korea. It was a great reunion. His wife and Marilyn immediately became friends. All of us enjoyed the historical sights. While visiting the pilgrim ship, Mayflower Two, Tim noticed a little man dressed in the garb of the Pilgrims. He walked right up to him and asked if he had come over on the Mayflower. We visited the famous Planetarium in Boston and the longest commissioned U. S. Naval ship, the Constitution.

Our hosts arranged for two nights stay for us at the famous Waldorf Astoria in New York. We could not afford meals in the hotel so we went down the street to Woolworth's lunch counter to eat. The next day we enjoyed Central Park, the Empire State Building, the Statue of Liberty and Times Square.

Washington D.C was something special. We camped in a lovely campground outside the city. As we were preparing our meal we noticed that the family next to us was singing Gospel songs. Introducing ourselves we made friends and enjoyed good fellowship together with this African American family.

From Washington D.C. we traveled through the hills of Virginia, up through Kentucky, Chicago and home via Montana visiting friends and many great sights. All along the way we held meetings sharing our experiences and raising support for the next term in Japan. In a small town north of Spokane we had just shown our film and spoken of the children we were reaching in Japan. An offering was taken for us. Among the bills and checks was an envelope. Sixteen dollars were in it along with a note asking us to use it to help the Japanese boys and girls know Jesus. It was signed in a young boy's hand. Looking up as I read it I noticed the boy and his mother standing there. The mother's eyes were moist as she related to me that the money was all the savings her ten year old had. He had been saving his money for a new bike. Instead he wanted to give it for the Lord's work, I am convinced that the Lord saw to it he got his bike. Our hearts were melted by this young lad's faith.

CHAPTER EIGHT

RETURN TO JAPAN

Sixteen months had passed since we arrived in Los Angeles. It was much too long. The Christian Academy in Japan was a full year ahead of schools here in the states. So our boys really repeated the last grade and missed the next. This caused problems for them in catching up. We decided our next furlough would only be four months over the summer.

When not on deputation I was on the staff of my home church in the position of Camp Director. This was good experience for our camps in Japan But our hearts were by then homesick for Japan

We once again boarded the plane in Seattle and flew over the pole to Tokyo. Our co-workers in JREF met us and we were back home in Nakagami Machi. We renewed friendships and took up old and new ministries. I was asked to be the English consultant for Tachikawa High School and soon began an English high school Bible class. These teens became close friends and good students.

VISITORS FROM HOME

Several friends and relatives visited us in Japan. Marilyn's father came to visit. His health was not good and his stay was short. During his visit I made arrangements to take him to the World's Fair held in Osaka some three hundred miles south. We bought tickets for the Bullet Train from Tokyo to Osaka. The Bullet Train was the world's fastest train at the time reaching speeds of two hundred kilometers an hour. This was much faster than an airplane because there was no boarding wait and the train went from city center to city center. Going at that speed took one's breath away. When we arrived in Osaka we went to an apartment some distance from the Fair Grounds. This apartment belonged to the company where one of my adult Bible students worked. We arrived at the local train station and hailed a cab. However, a Japanese anti-American group was demonstrating in front of the station. The cab driver was not sure he wanted to be seen with Americans. After much persuading he did take us and we settled in for the night. The next morning we took the local train to the Fair. It was huge covering a great many acres. Dad would tire easily so we frequently sat down on a bench. Each time we rested along the way to and from the exhibits I was approached by young Japanese friends who loudly and joyously greeted me. After this happened several times my father-in-law asked me if I knew *everybody* in Japan. I explained laughingly that I taught in an English language school in Tokyo and trained these young people for their positions as interpreters for the Fair. Dad was still puzzled and I think some what impressed.

A nephew and a couple ladies from one of our California churches came to visit also. At that time we were still living in the mountains. I was late getting the two ladies at their hotel and we had to hurry to the next train station, to catch our steam train to Karuizawa. I told the driver to really hurry. Traffic in Tokyo is bad enough, but when a cabby hurries it is terrifying. We made it to the station on time, but not before the ladies' faces were white. There was no room in the cars so we had to put our luggage between our feet and stand in the space between the rail cars with one foot on one car and the other foot on the other. The connection between the two cars moved up and down as it ran along the tract. Several hours later we arrived at our mountain village. By then the ladies were ready to sit down and rest. We always took our guests with us to Bible classes and Japanese church services as well as showing them the sights.

During Jan term at Whitworth College in Spokane my niece, Linda, spent the month of January with us. She would get credit for the essay she had to write about her experiences. It was a great visit. Taking her with me to Kyoto was exciting. It is the ancient capitol of Japan. When the "ships of death" arrived a couple hundred years ago they landed in Shimoda to make American presence known to the Emperor. However, foreign diseases were transmitted to the local populateion and thus they earned the name "ships of death.' The old Imperial Palace is there. Tokyo is the northern capitol and now the only one with its marvelous castle in the middle of downtown

In Kyoto there were many sights to see such as the Golden Pavilion, castles, Japanese gardens and many shrines and temples. At one shrine there was a pottery maker in the village. He was demonstrating his ancient art of molding tea cups. Bleachers were set around his work bench and kiln. He was working the clay effortlessly with his hands when all of a sudden he threw it back onto his bench. He explained that the clay was too hard to mold and needed more water. He thus started the wheel all over again. Finally he had a lovely Japanes tea cup. He put it in the kiln and asked us to return in a couple hours.

We walked around the area where small deer wandered among the croud. They were looking for handouts and often would stick their noses on one's pocket looking for nuts. Linda had some train schedules and other paper items in her pocket which one doe promptly chewed to pieces. There were little monkeys running all over the place. Wild Japanese monkeys can be dangerous and mean. One pinched Jerry real hard causing a bruise.

After a couple hours we returned to the pottery shop. The tea cup was finished and sitting on the bench. He handed it to one person and instructed her to pass it along and hold it up to the light and look through the bottom. Upon doing so we were amazed to see the image of the Crown Princess of Japan who is now the Empress. Later as Linda and I talked I was reminded of the Scripture relating how the Lord is the Potter and we are clay in His hand. Sometimes we are hard and resist His molding. He then has to "break" us and start over. His purpose of course is that when our lives are held up to the light others can see the image of His Son in us. It was a great lesson.

Soon it was time for Linda to leave and we returned to our various ministries in schools, rural areas, churches' After one crusade in northern Honshu, the largest Japanese Island, allowed us to take a few days vacation. We were staying with the pastor and his wife. They suggested we stay another day or so and visit Niko. Niko is one of the most famous National Parks of Japan. Alpine lakes with their clear blue water, contrasted with the fall colors made the view outstanding. When we arrived at the top the Japanese were having their annual parade of the Samurai. Wearing feudal costumes and mounted on magnificent horses these knights rode slowly through the ancient site to the delight of huge crowds. Nearby was a beautiful waterfall. Also a shrine dedicated to the many who had jumped over the falls to their deaths.

Returning to our hosts' house we took an very winding road down the mountain to the valley below. This trip was one of the highlights for any sightseer in Japan.

FOUR MONTHS THIS TIME

The four years of our second term had gone by too fast. Our family was growing. We now had four boys and it was time to report to our supporting churches. So it was that we sailed from Yokohama on the President Cleveland. This was a 24,000 ton vessel whereas the Brazil Maru was only 10,000 ton. It was a much smoother voyage then the first. This time the ship had a swimming pool and a cruise director just for the children. The boys had their own stateroom again and we ours. They were older now and got into more trouble by going into restricted areas of the ship where they were not supposed to be. The children had their own floor show to perform for the rest of us. Our boys and their cousin Tina were stars of that show. My brother, Lester, his wife and youngest daughter, Tina, met us in Honolulu to sail back to San Fransisco with us. This was the final world cruise that the President Cleveland would take. She was being sold to China Cruise Lines. This last portion of her world cruise was full of amenities and surprises. My brother and I held Bible classes. We were asked by the Captain to hold Sunday and Ash Wednesday services. Many attended and we had the opportunity of sharing the Gospel with them all. We had just four hours in Honolulu to see the sights. We all went to the Kodak Hula show and shopping. All nine of us purchased matching Hawaiian shirts and dresses. Upon returning aboard ship the deck officer commented that it was the first time a family left the ship and returned four hours later with three more members.

Arriving in San Francisco was the second time that I had ridden a ship under the San Francisco Bay Bridge. This was much better than the troop ship. Lester and family parted from us and flew home to Seattle. We took the boys and flew to Los Angeles to report to our churches there and picked up a pink Cadillac we had been given by one of our churches in San Diego. We also said a sad good bye to a lovely lady from Africa who raised lions. One of her lions was Ursula, from the movie *Born Free*. She delighted our boys with exciting tales and lovely pictures. Later we were to learn of her murder in Africa by a disgruntled employee.

We feverishly went from church to church in California reporting of our work, then drove home to Spokane to begin our furlough. We settled into a rental house across the street from Marilyn's mother and began our furlough. I had purchased a "See America" plane tour and spent six weeks flying around the United States for deputation meetings. It was a long and tiring trip. Returning to Spokane I spent the summer once again as the camp director at our church camp.

In the meantime Marilyn had her hands full with the four boys and summer events. Before we knew it we were preparing to return to Japan for our third term. This time we took Marilyn's mother, Trudy, with us. In those days pastors could fly on commuter airlines on stand-by for half the price. So we purchased full fare tickets for everyone but me. I was assured that there was room and once aboard I could not be removed from the plane until we got to our destination. This small plane landed in Yakima and picked up one passenger. He was one of the airline's executives. Immediately I was informed that I had to get off the plane. This was against the Airline policy, but he was a "big wig". I explained to the pilot and this man that I would miss my flight to Tokyo and my family would go on without me. There was not another flight from Yakima to San Francisco for twenty four hours. Argue as I may this man would not give in. I reminded him that the rules said that after I boarded I could not be removed in flight. But there was no moving him and no attempt to understand my predicament. Then a man sitting part way back came up and offered his seat. Knowing that he could not get out of Yakima for twenty four hours he was willing to do what the airline executive would not. Again the Lord had intervened and we were on our way.

We all stayed the night with our friends in San Francisco and boarded a China Airlines flight for Tokyo the next day. We had a very luxurious flight. It was topped only several years later by a flight from Moscow, Russia to Onck, Siberia. Our fellow missionaries met us and drove us home to Nakagami. Mom was excited over all the new sights and smells. Masa's sister took Mom to Yokohama for a weekend. Another Japanese friend took her to see Kyoto. I had injured my back and had to take things easy so I had time to ferry Mom around. I took her to give her testimony at one of my home churches. With me interpreting she really enjoyed that experience. She stayed through Christmas and then returned to Spokane with a lot of memories and stories to tell.

The next spring, only eight months into our third furlough, things drastically changed. Marilyn had a serious curvature of the spine due to Scoliosis. We noticed that our son Tim's back was not straight. A trip to the doctor and exrays taken showed serious progressive scoliosis We called Dr. Adamson our mission doctor (and my former CO in Korea). He practiced in Boston. His partner's husband was one of America's leading specialists in scoliosis. He had us take ex-rays of the other boys, except John. All showed progressive scoliosis. I had already put Tim on my passport preparing for me to return with him to the states immediately. We soon found out that adequate immediate treatment was not afforded us in Tokyo. In addition by now our Mission doctor urged us to all return home stating that Tim would probably need extensive surgery. If not, then a full torso brace for his growing years. As it turned out both Tim and Jerry needed the braces. The other two boys were able to get by with daily specific exercises. It was this decision that had prompted Kazanori's visit .

We put our things in storage, gave Frank power of attorney, and our hanko, a round piece of wood with our name carved in the end. This was stamped in wax on each document and served as our personal legal signature. Thus whomever had our "hanko" could buy and sell for us. We were preparing in case we could not return. In that case Frank could sell our house for us and terminate any business we had left to do.

The Japanese yen was fluctuating in regard to the U.S. dollar. When we brought dollars into Japan we had to buy yen at the current rate of 270 yen per dollar. But when be bought our airline tickets we had to pay the official rate of 360 yen per dollar, thus loosing value right away. Our Christian travel agent arranged for us to buy tickets only to Guam in Japanese yen. In Guam, an American possession, we could use dollars to purchase tickets for the rest of the trip. It was a good move as we saved nearly $400 that way. We flew to Guam from a cool Tokyo in April only to arrive in mid-afternoon in sweltering heat. Guam was beautiful with blue lagoons and quaint villages. A twenty four hour layover gave us time to see the little island. The hotel was like one seen in the movie, *Key Largo* with slowly moving ceiling fans. Our short stay was spoiled by John getting severly ill. We spent most of the next morninig in the doctor's office. Later we did get to drive around the island and swam in the lagoon The boys had to wear tennis shoes because of the coral.

The next day we boarded a Pan Am flight for Honolulu. Very few were on the plane so our family took a full row of seats across the center of the plane. We had just passed the no return point when we noticed smoke in the cabin. Stewardesses ran around with fire extinguishers and terrified expressions on ther faces. The fire seemed to be in the wiring in the right side of the fuselage. Soon the pilot turned off all power to that side and activated fire extinguishers inside the skin of the airplane. We were relieved to find that we were not going to ditch in the middle of the Pacific ocean. We landed as if there had never been a problem. Renting a nice Ford LTD we checked into our hotel on Waikiki Beach. The $400 saved would purchase four days and three nights there. We were right on the beach, however on the eleventh floor of the high-rise hotel. It was dinner and shopping at the International Bazaar in Honolulu. The next day we drove around Diamond Head and swam at Hanauma Bay. Here Steve got stung by a bumble bee much to his disgust. In the next couple days we drove to Hawaii's Sea World and then to the Polynesian Village. This was great. It was so hot that John couldn't eat his ice-cream cone fast enough and it dripped all over him.

Four wonderful vacation days over we flew on to Seattle. We had seventeen bags of luggage among the six of us. Lester met us and took us to his home while we looked for a place to live. Numerous medical appointments were arranged to get the boys started on their scoliosis treatment. Tim was told he would avoid surgery if he would be extremely careful to follow all instructions and wear the brace faithfully which he did for five years. West Side Presbyterian Church, my home church in high school, offered their empty manse to us and we finally settled down, not really knowing what the future would hold.

PART II

CHAPTER NINE

THE DREAM ENDS

GOD'S PLANS, NOT OURS

All my life I had wanted to be a missionary. This was also Marilyn's dream. But dreams have a way of ending. When Marilyn grabbed my hand those many years ago as we first sat foot in Japan and said, "Honey, we're home," our plan was until we die in our land of calling. I am glad that we do not know the future, but God does. That makes faith all the more exciting. Unforeseen circumstances pop up and plans change. But God's overall plan for our lives does not change. He knows the future from the beginning.

Now it was our responsibility to find out what those future plans were. After the boys were through with their treatment, would we return to Japan? But that would be

years away. Do I look for a secular job? What would I do?
I could not go back to the dairy industry. Do I go back
to school? Do I seek a pastorate? Questions, questions
and no answers

In the meantime we settled into the manse at West
Side and began teaching an adult class. The older boys
entered Seattle Christian School. Even John was old
enough already for kindergarten. His aunt Margaret
taught the kindergarten class there. It was a fun time.
Summer was soon upon us and we bought a tiny camping
trailer. We took off to spots around Puget Sound to get as
much family time as we could.

Our support from the mission would soon end and
we had to do something. Meanwhile we enjoyed our time
at West Side Presbyterian Church,.

OUR WEST SIDE STORY

When my father and I moved to Seattle after my mother's
death we joined the West Side Presbyterian Church in
West Seattle. Now upon returning from the mission field
I took my family and returned to West Side. The reunion
was great. Many old friends were there including high
school buddies and friends. It seemed that time had not
moved at all. The church very kindly offered us the manse
which had been empty for some time. It was a little small
for our family, but clean and adequate. Soon the boys
were enrolled in Seattle Christian School and we settled
in.

The first order of business was to get the boys medical attention for their scoliosis. This was done quickly and Timothy and Jerry were fitted for Milwaukee braces. These were awkward devices custom-made for each individual and covering the entire torso. It had pressure areas to counteract the curvature and hold their spines steady. How to pay for all this? The Lord supplied once again. Gifts from relatives and supporters came in to cover the cost of the braces which was significant.

Second on the health list was myself. I had been having urinary problems for some time. Now I had a thorough check-up which revealed a significant tumor on the prostate. Since it was not an emergency a down payment was required by the hospital. We borrowed some of the payment from a kind lady in Spokane and the rest the Lord supplied in various ways. The doctor provided his services and the surgery was a success. After a brief time in the hospital I came home to the manse to recuperate. Our wedding anniversary came and my brother and his wife took the boys with them so we could have a nice evening together. During dinner I found that I could not urinate. I was getting worried so I called the doctor. He figured that there was a blood clot in the bladder and instructed me to drink several glasses of water to flush it out. That did not work. The excess water was stretching my bladder so that I was in great discomfort. Another call and an ambulance was summoned which rushed me back to the hospital, It was a busy June night with no beds available except in the maternity ward. They removed the clot through catheterization and settled me in my room. Needless to say when the new mothers saw me on their ward, they were surprised. Proper explanation was given and I laid back to go to sleep. Later that evening my heart began to race at nearly 300 beats per minute. I mentioned it to the nurse who checked my heart with her stethoscope and called for a crash cart. They rushed me to the emergency room and called Marilyn. Our pastor brought Marilyn to me shortly. By then my heart had converted back to its normal beat. A couple more days of observation in the hospital and I came home. There went our anniversary dinner.

My recovery was swift and we spent the rest of the summer camping along the shores of beautiful Puget Sound. I ministered in the church as much as was needed. Still there was no answer as to what the Lord wanted me to do. We just waited on Him.

Steve was very athletic so we enrolled him in a ballet and gymnastics school near Green Lake. The students were mostly girls for ballet. Steve was the only boy gymnastic student. The couple running the school were Russian and had danced in the Russian Ballet. He saw great potential in Steve. When he found out we were moving he begged us to stay saying that Steve was Olympic Games material. However we knew how shy Steve was and doubted he would like the attention that went with that sport.

We had purchased a little Cavalier King Charles spaniel for Steve in Japan which he named Keiko. She was a very cute little dog. Steve and the boys loved to run along the beach with Keiko chasing after them. June went by as did July. In August we received a visit from Pastor Ed and an elder from Fourth Memorial Church in Spokane. They wanted to know if I might be interested in the position of camp director at Riverview Bible Camp. This was the camp the church owned sixty miles north of Spokane. Since I had been in camp ministry in Japan we thought that we should consider this opening for the Lord's service. After much prayer and assurances from the boys' doctor that Spokane had fine doctors in the orthopedic field there, we accepted and began packing for the move.

We soon moved into Marilyn's mother's home in Spokane and began looking for a house. There was a lovely little home for sale in north Spokane. Not really big enough, but it would make do. Arranging for a VA loan we purchased it and squeezed into the little two-bedroom house. The basement was soon divided into another bedroom and we settled in.

By now our missionary support had ceased. It was comforting to know we would have a regular pay check.

CHAPTER TEN

MILLIONS OF YEN

BOXES OF MONEY

Much excitement filled our home as we made preparations to leave Seattle. There were school records to obtain, doctor's advice for the boys, packing again and moving. Tim was by now getting used to his Milwaukee brace. It had two "wings" that held his head high, braces on the back to hold the spine in place and leather hip rests. Jerry had to wait until we got to Spokane to receive his brace. My own health was not the best following the last surgery. Many concerns for the future still lingered.

I interned at Riverview the rest of the summer, learning all I could about being a camp director. Sundays I taught an adult class of about 300 people. It was like a small church within a large one.

Marilyn's sister, Joan, offered us her basement to live in while we were looking to buy a home. We found a nice little one and bought it with a VA loan. That very summer TEAM missionary friends from Japan stopped by in their trailer and stayed a few days while he did deputation work in the area. My brother and family came to visit just as the snow arrived. It was so bad they were stuck here for a few days not able to get over the pass to Seattle.

With the secure income we begin to spend more than we should. Credit cards were new to us and we did not know how to manage them. With a steady income we could work out a budget. However, we missed the days when we had to depend totally on the Lord's supply. It was too easy to depend on people than the Lord

Pastor Ed and I left Spokane for a conference in Boise, Idaho. The second day I received a frantic phone call from Marilyn. Our house in Japan had been sold and the money shipped to us in cash in two cardboard boxes. What to do? I contacted my brother in Seattle who I in turn contacted the International Monetary Exchange. They stated a set price if we could get the money to them that afternoon before closing time. The dollar was still fluctuating with regards to the yen and the quote was only good for a few hours. Our church had a band of retired men we called "Minute Men". They were charged to carry out needed tasks upon first notice. Charlie agreed to carry the money on the plane to Seattle where he would hand it to my brother, who would rush it to the Exchange. Since it was in Japanese yen there were bundles of brand new 10,000 yen notes which numbered in the thousands of yen. Marilyn put them in a small suitcase and drove Charlie to the airport. He was on standby. His name was called and he hurried through the inspection line. In those days there were no x-ray machines so every bag had to be opened. When the guard opened the bag she saw all that money, sacks of 10,000 yen notes. "How much is there?" she inquired. Speaking of yen, not dollars, Charlie replied that there were several million. Thinking dollars the clerk nearly fainted. But all was well and she handed the suitcase back to Charlie who grabbed it and headed toward the concourse. However, she had not latched the suit case. It flung open and stacks of ten thousand yen bills fell onto the floor. Retrieving them quickly Charlie ran down the concourse to the waiting plane. Marilyn could see the plane on the tarmac, the stewardess waiting uneasily. Several minutes went by before Charlie appeared with the suitcase. When he returned he mentioned that at the end of the concourse several customs agents were waiting for him. It took a while to persuade them that everything was legitimate.

A few days later we received a check for over $50,000 dollars. The house had sold for nearly $100,000, but after Japanese taxes, real estate fees and commissions it only produced a little over $50,000. But that was more than we had ever seen. We had ninety days to buy another house to avoid heavy U.S. taxes.

We used a quit-claim deed to turn the current house over to a young couple in the church who took over my VA loan. Then we went house hunting, It was really exciting as we had to spend it all on house and furnishings or pay heavy taxes. We looked for days and finally bought a show house in the Brentwood area near the Mead High School. It had six bedrooms, two and one half baths with the master bedroom closet bigger than our entire bedroom in Japan. We furnished it with nice furniture and had everything put in place. The builder framed the basement family room, two bedrooms and a bath. Marilyn's uncle Dave, a carpenter finished everything off so we had a beautiful home. Since we paid cash for the home there was no mortgage. The Lord had indeed showered blessing upon blessing on us. Some members of the church were critical of our having such a nice house not realizing that to do otherwise was to give much of the money from the sale of our Tokyo house to the government. That was not good stewardship.

The boys were soon patients at the Shrine Children's Hospital in Spokane. It was another of God's gifts to us as there was no charge. Marilyn would take them to the hospital several days a week for treatment. There we met the doctor who would become a good friend over the years and perform scoliosis surgery on Marilyn years later. It was a difficult time as I was away in camp ministry. It became Marilyn's responsibility to care for the children including their daily exercises.

The boys entered public school. It was strange for Tim and Jerry. Students and teachers did not always understand about the brace. In one class the teacher was determined that disabled children would receive no special treatment. So when Tim ask for a table and chair to replace the seat-desk, he was refused. The problem was that the wing's on his brace forced him to look up and if he could not push his chair back he could not see the chalk board or teacher. One of the first days some boys knocked Tim's books out of his hand onto the floor. Tim could not bend over with the brace on. He had to get on his knees to retrieve his books. He later said that it was a good lesson as he would have to put with bullies for the next five years. The matter of the desk had not be resolved. A friend from the church paid full tuition for all four boys at Northwest Christian School and from then on things were fine.

RIVERVIEW

George Pontius...
An inspiration to everyone at Camp!

Becoming the director of a large Bible camp such as Riverview was much more than I had bargained for. Camps in Japan were small in number and area. Choices of recreation were few consisting mainly of hiking, swimming in the ocean or pool and volleyball. Riverview, however, was large and one of the finest in the Northwest. We had a capacity of 150 campers plus staff. Being located on a bend of a very large river we had water skiing, swimming, and canoeing, Bible classes were taught in the mornings, vespers in the evening, camp fires, films and lots of fun fishing, barbecues and cookouts. During my time there we built a gymnasium big enough for double basketball courts. We purchased a huge gunny sack slide and the care-taker's son built the River Queen paddle wheeler. There was a warm swimming pool, cold swimming in the river, volley ball court and baseball field. Camp counselors were gleaned from our church and others. The speakers were top notch and the adult retreats inspiring. Baptisms were held each Labor Day in the river. Pastor Ed and I on one such occasion baptized over fifty believers in one afternoon. There were many spiritual victories won at Riverview.

As I look back at my years at Riverview many good memories stand out. Often we would load the campers in the buses and go to a cave on the adjacent Indian Reservation. This cave had been hewn out for meetings. There was a stone altar and bleachers carved in the stone of the cave. The Lord's supper was served there. It was a wonderfully spiritual atmosphere with only candle light inside and the darkness outside.

On another occasion on a New Years eve just before we served communion I challenged everyone to set relationships right with each other and the staff before taking communion. It was very quiet. Then one by one the kids got up, went to each other and asked forgiveness. Standing in the back was a missionary home from the field. One of the campers was his teenage son. They had been estranged and fighting. I saw this young man go to his father, ask forgiveness together and hug him. These were the highlights as well as the camp fires, testimonies and redemptions.

One year I had the privilege of having three young men on my staff all of whom are in full time ministry now. Early in the morning we would go to the ball field and spend time together in prayer for that day's spiritual activities.

It was at Riverview that I learned the truth that all ministry is the Lord's, not ours. Letting Him lead brings great Spiritual results. Insisting on my own way does not. The intensity of the work and the many well-meaning demands were beginning to take their toll. I was on the road to defeat. There would come a time when my personal "dungeon" would be opened and I would be forced deal with the past.

CHAPTER ELEVEN

A MATTER OF REPENTANCE

Andrew Murray once said that opposite great heights are the deepest depths. He was right. Enjoying the success of Riverview I failed to maintain my own spiritual life. My devotional and prayer life went down the tube. Soon I was out of touch with the Lord and the power of the Holy Spirit had departed. I became angry as I was criticized frequently over misunderstandings and incidental things. Things were falling apart in my life My behavior reached a head one day and it was obvious that I needed to resign my pastoral position.

During that time Marilyn's own scoliosis had reached a critical point and she decided it was time for radical surgery. She consulted the doctor that our children had at Shriners Childrens Hospital. After much discussion she prepared for this major surgery. A plaster cast was applied to her entire torso. She was put on a "stretching" apparatus which straightened her spine as much as possible without tearing the muscles and ligaments. Immediately the plaster was applied. A month or so later the doctor removed the cast and operated. The surgery took nearly nine hours. They split open every vertebrae from the second cervical to the tenth thoracic. From her hips they removed bone chips and lined each open vertebrae with them. A Harrington rod about the size of her little finger at least thirteen inches long was inserted at the top and bottom, holding the curvature at that point. Finally the vertebrae were stapled shut and the spine fused in that position. This type of surgery has the most painful recovery of all. Marilyn was in a state of confusion for several days. She was the first adult to have this surgery in Spokane. The nursing staff did not believe she was in the amount of pain she was. Our doctor took a vacation after the grueling surgery. I was informed by a staff member that she was not being handled carefully when moved causing extreme pain. She recommended that I come stay with her 24-7. We had been in counseling with a great psychaitrist whom I then called. He immediately came and rectified the situation. The night staff was replaced and I was permitted to stay with her all day and night. While we were in Japan President Kennedy was assassinated. We were all put on alert in case the communist faction might take advantage of this and kidnap some hostages. During her early recovery Marilyn reverted to that time thinking she had been captured and was being tortured. She motioned for me to come close so she could whisper. Her words were very soft as she told me that she would not deny Christ no matter what "they" did. That brought me to tears. Slowly she began to get better. A full torso cast was applied and she was able to come home. That cast remained for about six months and was replaced by a plastic cast she could remove for showers or a swim. It had holes in it also so air could reach her skin. It would be a full year before it was removed permanently

DEALING WITH FAILURE

"And you have forgotten that the word of encouragement that addresses you as sons.

> 'My son, do not make light of the
>   Lord's discipline,
> and do not lose heart when He
>   rebukes you,
> because the Lord disciplines those He
>   loves,
> and He punishes everyone He
>   accepts as a son'." Hebrews 12:5-6 (NIV)

When God brings you to the point where He forces you to deal with your rebellion it is seldom that the encouragement of these words in Hebrews take hold. However, though the inner pain was deep, and the fear of rejection was beyond grasp, God's dealing with me was a release so that I could begin dealing with the past. The door of the dungeon I had built in my heart from childhood began to crack open.

Having resigned from the church I accepted the forgiveness of the Lord and others. However, I could not forgive myself. I had made a mess of things. Marilyn had suffered physically beyond my understanmding. Rebuilding my relationship with the Lord, my family and the church would take years to accomplish. I was determined to do so. The church offered a watch care group which I readily accepted. Dr. "Nick" Faber became my dear friend and counselor. Slowly we began to explore the dungeon that still lay hidden deep within.

SURVIVING THE STORM

My church was most gracious and though we had resigned they provided me with salary for six months until I could find a way to make a living while I was healing from it all. It was imperative that I take many months and even a couple years to rebuild spiritually, emotionally and relationally.

Using my skills as a Navy Medical Corpsman, I obtained a position as a Nurse's Aide at a local nursing home. The pay was minimal. My skills were well above other aides so I was given more responsibility. It was not a nice place to work, though the patients were most needy.

In the meantime I began my own business with a company that sold product to distributors who in turn either sold them or used them in their own business. I began to work with a roof coating. However, I received little to no training. In addition I was not good at business. I supplemented this by working at night for an electronics company building computer components. This did not work, so I quit to give full time to the business. Because of the lack of training and skill at running a business I soon lost nearly everything I had. We had to sell our lovely home with the swimming pool in order to pay off creditors from the business. We subsequently moved to another new, but much less expensive home, being able to pay cash again.

At this time I learned of the Evangelical Lutheran Good Samaritan home in Fairfield, Washington. A position opened for an activity director. It was almost seventy miles away. The driving was too much. So several days a week I stayed in our camping trailer which I had parked at the nursing home. In the meantime Marilyn and I were working on our Masters Degrees at Whitworth College. She graduated with a Masters of Education in Reading and Special Education and I a Masters of Education in Counseling and Guidance. We both were working. She was a teachers aide though she was State Certified. It was frustrating for her when she could not get a teaching position. I was then "promoted" to Social Worker and Chaplain at the nursing home in Fairfield. Of course the business had failed and we had to move again to the home in which we now live. Our two oldest children graduated from high school, Steve to work and Tim to the Navy where he eventually joined the Submarine Force both with the Atlantic and Pacific fleets.

I continued at Good Sam where the work was rewarding. The residents were much appreciative. It was a joy to take them places in the van, to counsel them, and minister to their spiritual needs. Sunday worship services offered me the opportunity to renew my ministerial skills. One of the volunteers mentioned that her church was in need of a new pastor. It had been three years since I had left the ministry. Meeting with my accountability committee at my home church we decided it was time to return to the pastorate. I applied for the position as pastor at this rural church.. It was time to begin another phase of our lives.

CHAPTER TWELVE

CLIMBING UP AGAIN

IN CHRIST EVERYONE
IS SOMEONE

This was the stated theme of the Good Samaritan Centers. I really liked the concept. Even after becoming pastor of this rural church Marilyn and I continued ministering to people in nursing homes. I was called by a nursing home on the lower south hill of Spokane. It was late evening when the phone rang informing me that a lady I had been ministering too was about to pass away. I rushed to the home to be with her. It had been my determination when I first began working in nursing homes that if at all possible I would never let anyone die alone. She was a long time friend and member of one of my Bible classes. It was about 2 a.m. when I arrived in her room. She had slipped into a coma. I took her hand in one of mine. Remembering that she loved the poem, "Footprints In the Sand," I whispered in her ear. "Can you see the footprints in the sand? Jesus is coming for you." She squeezed my hand as I continued, "He is reaching out for you. Reach out for Him. Take His hand and go with Him." Then I gently transferred her hand from one of mine to the other. She immediately relaxed, sighed and entered glory. I sat there holding her hand for some time. When the tears quit flowing I went to inform the staff that she was gone. No wonder the Word says that the death of a saint is precious in the eyes of the Lord.

BACK PACKING AND SUCH

The ministry was at first wonderful. We organized a youth group, and a Boy's Brigade scout group. Campouts were exciting teaching them scouting skills and the Word of God. Our leaders were excellent. It was at this time my son, Tim, introduced me to back packing On several occasions we took campers high into the mountains of the North Idaho Panhandle. On one such trip we were camped at about 8,000 feet. Our plans were to have spaghetti for dinner. However, we had forgotten that at that altitude spaghetti does not boil. The result was a gooey mess no one could eat. So we left it for the bears. The next year it was still on the ground as even the animals would not eat it. On another back pack trip Tim and I had only three high school boys with us. We hiked further to Blossom lake, raised our tents and settled in for a great weekend. However, soon the clouds came and the rain poured. We put a plastic cover over the area, including the fire pit where we remained the entire day while the rain continued. That night as we were snuggled in our sleeping bags the weather turn nasty and cold. Waking up in the morning we found ourselves in several inches of snow. It was mid-July and we were not prepared for winter camping. It was immediately clear we had to break camp and get out. The trail back to our vehicles climbed another thousand feet before it traversed its way down the mountains. One of the boys did not want to leave, but we had to. We were hungry as we left the mountain without breakfast. So we stopped in Kellogg, Idaho to eat. The one boy who was up set that we cut the trip short refused to come into the restaurant to eat. He sat in the pickup truck sulking while we ate pancakes and drank coffee. We said nothing. It was his empty stomach and his choice.

PROBLEMS, PARENTS
AND PASTORS

When we are determined to hold forth the truth of God's Word without compromise Satan gets upset. His method often is to use wolves in sheep's clothing out of your own flock to do his work. In this case it was the teaching staff of our school. The main teacher had problems with men and in particular with my oversight of the school. She began to spread untruths behind my back. This tactic worked. I found myself defending my every move, not realizing until later that it was all lies and a set up. She brought non-Christian students into the school without my knowledge. One morning she told me that the aunt of a couple students had died and requested that I talk to the boys and inform them. What she did not tell me was that the parents that very morning had asked her not to tell the boys but that they would inform them when school as out. She set me up. So thinking that the parents wanted me to speak to them I did so. Then she told the parents that I would not honor their wishes and went ahead and had spoken to the boys. Immediately I received a very angry phone call from the parents. Taking a couple of my Elders with me I rushed to the home to explain. However, they would not listen and using terrible language and swearing they assailed me. My Elders, however, did nothing to quiet the situation. Finally I told them that if they were not going to listen at all to me and just continue to yell and swear at me there was no point in my remaining and I abruptly left. I was in turmoil and tears. Needing some understanding and comfort I called a close friend in the church. But, I made a big mistake and got a hold of someone else. Before I realized my mistake I had blurted out the problem. This person was kind to my face, but immediately called the gossip ladies in the church.

The teacher called a meeting of all the staff and parents. The parents had been told all her lies as truth. During the course of the meeting I was not allowed to speak. I objected and demanded to be heard. At that point one parent attacked me physically and nearly knocked me down.

A few weeks later the congregation voted to close the school. The staff was free to take all the equipment once they found another place. However, shortly the same problem arose in their new church setting and the school was closed permanently.

There was a core of strong believers who were trying to change the doctrinal tone to be more Bible centered. This was opposed by several women who informed me that they had been in the church long before I came and they would remain long after I was gone.

The discord had been sown so deep that the end was inevitable. Immediately after a morning service I was terminated without any compensation. A really nice young man was hired. He too was Gospel and youth oriented. However on the eve of his wedding these same ladies gave him a similar note of dismissal to be effective immediately.

During the whole experience I was reminded of the warning the Lord's Word gives us: "Six things do I hate, saith the Lord, …a lying tongue, feet swift to shed blood… and the seventh is an abomination to Me, he that soweth discord among the brethren." Proverbs 6:14 (KJV)

CHAPTER THIRTEEN

DARE WE TRY AGAIN?

GOD'S SUPPLY

Again the Lord fulfilled His promise to us to supply our needs. When I was a youth pastor in my days at Biola College I met a young man, then only thirteen years old. I have mentioned Fred Martin before. Over the years he had grown in the faith, graduated from Bible College, served as youth pastor of Central Bible Church, his home church, and was now a Pastor near Portland, Oregon. Having learned that I was looking for another ministry he wrote to me that the a church in south Spokane was in need of a new pastor and suggested that I interview for the position. I did so and was asked to become their new pastor. Soon I was installed and began my pastoral work at a local church in Spokane.

It was an older church with a strong Biblical base. It had a strong evangelical background. The leadership was firmly in place. There is always a honeymoon period in every pastorate. We enjoyed getting to know and love the people. It was especially wonderful to be able to freely declare the truths of God's Word with encouragement. All the ministries of the church such as Sunday School, Ladies groups, men's fellowship and Vacation Bible School were well established. In the early weeks I traveled to the denomination's headquarters in the Chicago area for orientation. There I learned that my new church had some internal problems specifically when it came to youth and to change. It was in danger of dying. I was encouraged to reach out to today's youth and young couples in order to save the church from extinction. Much of the problem lay with the leadership and women. There were certain cliques within the congregation. Newcomers to the church were not really welcomed as they were seen as a threat to the established control and form of worship. Nothing was to be done without "so-and-so's" approval. This issue over control has caused the death of many an older church.

When I returned from Chicago I realized the truth of what I learned there. There were only two or three teenagers in the church. This congregation had somehow lost their own children's interest in their church. This weighed heavily on Marilyn and me as we had always emphasized the need of a strong youth ministry. We asked the church to pray about this. So we prayed and waited for the Lord's direction.

A KNOCK AT THE DOOR

The only office of the church served as the pastor's office and was located in the rear of the church behind the platform, far away from the main door. I had no secretary and was usually alone at the church when I was in the office. One day I heard a distant, but persistent rapping on the main door of the church. Upon opening it I was surprised to come face to face with a sixteen year old boy. Here was the answer to our prayers, I thought. "Do you have a youth group?", he asked. Quickly gathering my thoughts I told him that we did not, but if he and some friends wanted to come next Wednesday evening at seven 7 p.m. I would be there. All day Wednesday I wondered if he would actually show up. With great hope I prepared the dining area in the basement for the youth meeting. We were praying as were many members. Sharply at seven p.m. he arrived. With this young lad were about fifteen other teens. I was astonished, but joyful. What to do, teach a Bible class, preach? No that was not the answer. Getting to know them first was. I asked each one to give a short history about themselves and why they were here.

Each one did so. As I listened my heart filled with sadness and concern over the tragedies of many of their lives. Many of these kids were literally street kids. Their backgrounds were full of horrible experiences of rejection and lack of love. As there had been dungeon experiences in my life, so there were in theirs. Not all of them of course. Some of them were from good homes, but homes that lacked knowledge of God. Curiosity had brought them, led by this sixteen year old boy. I immediately became vulnerable and mentioned the spiritual struggles of my own youth. The Holy Spirit led me to identify with them and their struggles. Shortly the bond of Christian love brought a cohesiveness to the group as many heard for the first time that God did love them most deeply. They were in much need for His love. Forgiveness was a new concept to many. Relating the Gospel story brought tears to several eyes.

Thus began our youth group. It grew to over fifty kids. New adults began to investigate the church. Sunday morning attendance increased significantly with many youth attending. Hope seemed to be pounding at the door.

A BACKPACK NEVER FORGOTTEN

With the growth of the Sunday School, Vacation Bible School and youth group we soon realized that transportation to all these events was a problem. A small church bus became available and the church purchased it. Back packing camps were a favorite of mine and my son, Tim. As our own boys were growing up we spent lots of summers camping, hiking and playing as a family. As adults the boys also kept up the tradition. Tim was and is a teacher in northeast Washington state with his home atop a small mountain. He had introduced me to back packing and volunteered to help me organize several back packing adventures. For this first back pack trip for this group I took Tim and my grandson, Craig, to investigate a neat spot. In the Idaho panhandle, deep in the mountains are twin lakes, Upper and Lower Stevens Lakes. The road to the trail was filled with ruts and rocks, but looked like it was passable for the bus. We parked our cars at the foot of the trail where an abandoned mine left room to park and turn around. The trail was very steep, through alpine forests, steep climbs, flowering meadows and finally a nice waterfall just before we stumbled upon the lakes. Several camping spots were large enough for back packing tents with a larger area for group meetings. This was indeed the spot.

We had invited two other churches to join us with their youth groups. Marilyn went along, a first for her, as did our missionary to Africa, a doctor who was on furlough. Altogether there were about thirty of us painstakingly trudging our way up the mountain. Some places were so steep we had to grab onto branches to help pull ourselves up. Each hiker carried a pack with sleeping gear and eating utensils. Food was distributed among all of us, except Marilyn because of her back. One boy however, snuck a large can of fruit into her pack. We soon found that trick and it was returned to him to carry. After we set up our tents in various areas, designated toilet areas and prepared the group spot we were ready to eat. It fell to Dr. Helen and Marilyn to do much of the cooking. While dinner was being prepared over a small camp fire the kids explored the area. From the lower lake the trail dwindled and was hard to find, so we lost no one going very far from the camp area. Most of the youth had never been in the wilderness before. The howling wolves and sounds of bears and other animals in the forest made the first night exciting.

The second day was a Saturday. The sixteen year old who had first knocked on the church door came to me and asked to be baptized in the lake. He had cleared it with his parents, both nominal Roman Catholics, who were happy to see their son's spiritual growth. I counseled with him for some time and decided to have the baptism the next morning near the group area just before our worship service was to begin.

The rest of the day was given to swimming in the cold waters, fishing, visiting, hiking and of course eating. With us were the youth leaders from the other two churches and Tim. Each were assigned to an evening vesper or Bible study and the Sunday morning worship service. Evening campfires are always special. Our singing echoed off the mountain cliffs nearby. The fire sent an eerie glow on the water and the times of silence were awesome. The Word of God was making way in the hearts and minds of the kids.

That youth leader of the First Baptist Church in Colfax, Washington was scheduled to lead the Sunday morning service. I encouraged him to do so but he insisted that I bring the message.

Early on Sunday morning we were awakened by the noise of other hikers coming up the trail. They turned out to be several fishermen who had come for the big trout in the lake. We greeted everyone. They were surprised to see so many youth so high in the mountains. Our bus had been parked at the trail head which caused them to wonder. Soon they were lining the shore, casting their fishing lines into the lake. We all went about our morning routine and breakfast before gathering for the baptism and worship service. Our singing broke through the air in melody. Soon we noticed that the fishermen had come closer so they could listen. The lad being baptized gave a strong testimony of his new found faith. With everyone listening and watching, including the fishermen, I explained that water baptism was an illustration of being buried with Christ and rising again to new life. All were silent as he and I climbed out of the lake.

Next was the worship service. More singing and then the sermon. During the night I had contemplated on what to speak about. Remembering the spiritual warfare we endured both in Japan and at the rural church the Lord led me to speak on the reality of the power of the Holy Spirit and of Satan's spiritual forces. I related the advice of one of my theology professors at Biola. "Gentleman," he said, "If you remember nothing else, remember this. Do not relegate the power of the Holy Spirit or the power of Satan to the first century." I then went on to speak of the spiritual battles we all would face and entreated each one to join in that battle committing to Christ on a daily basis.

CONFRONTED BY DEMONS

That particular Sunday was hot. By the time we climbed down from the mountain, got on the church bus and arrived in Spokane it was in the 90's. We dropped off our kids at my church and proceeded to the next little town for gas. We still had some thirty miles to go to Colfax to deliver the last of our campers and their youth leader. The third group had come from Montana so went east from the camp to go home. There was only one gas station in this town. I was known to many there as I had been the pastor there for some time. The heat was sweltering as we pulled up to the pump. As I reached for the pump a very angry man came up in his pickup and yelled, "You, get your @#!+ hands off that pump. I want it." "I am sorry," I replied "we were here first." Looking into his fiery eyes I realized that soft words were better and continued, "However, if you are in a hurry I will move and you can go first." "You bet I will," he shouted. I moved the bus and waited for him to finish filling his tank. He scowled at me while he pumped his gas. "It's always the same with you preachers," he spurted out. "We got rid of you once. We are determined to keep it that way. We know who you are and you and your kind will not be able to speak your lies here again. We will see to that." I replied quietly, knowing that it was a demon causing him to make these threats. "God loves you, you know," I said. "Don't say that," he shouted. "Jesus loves you," I repeated. With a curse he put the nozzle in the pump, got in and drove to store to pay for the gas.

I drove up to the pump and began to fill the tank. All windows were open and the back emergency door so that everyone aboard heard the exchange. Finished I had the youth pastor from Colfax go into the store to pay. "Pastor, here comes that guy," one of the boys yelled. The man got into his pickup and started the engine moving toward me. "Lookout," the kids in the bus screamed. I jumped out of the way as the truck stopped suddenly. Getting out of the truck he came at me with a tire iron in his hand. For a moment I did not know what to do. Remembering our experience in Japan with demons I shouted at him as my theology professor had told me to do in such situations. "By the power of the name of Jesus stop." Immediately he dropped his hand and returned to the truck. I approached the driver's window. It was then I noticed two women seated in the truck with alarmed looks on their faces. I put my hand on the window edge of the door. "You know God really does love you." His eyes lost their anger and he relaxed embarrassed and leaned his head back on the seat. He then sat up, looked me in the eyes and declared, "You really believe that @#*! Don't you?" "Yes, I do." I replied. He was silent for a few seconds before he surprised me by saying, "Well, I had better think about that." Putting the truck in gear he slowly drove out of the station and into town. I wondered who he was as I had not seen him before.

After I boarded the bus again and the doors were closed someone asked me, "what was that all about?" It took nearly another hour to get to Colfax. On the way I reminded them of what I had said in the sermon that morning at camp. We Christians are in a daily battle with the forces of evil. Even now as I write this in the summer

174

of 2010, the world has fast moved to deny Christ and Satan is about to establish his antichrist rule.

As we were unloading the campers and their gear in Colfax several boys came to talk and pray. They all stated that they were willing to trust the Lord for strength for the battles ahead. I have never seen them again. But I hear from their youth director about their good spiritual progress. I thought that was the end of Satan's attack on us that day, but I was wrong.

While we were in the mountains the youth pastor's wife had left Colfax to go to Clarkston, Washington several miles down the Lewiston grade. Her parents lived there where her father was a pastor. She was due home by seven that evening but had not arrived. We waited for her return. She did not arrive until about ten that night. Immediately it was clear by the look in her eyes that something horrible had happened. Tearfully she related that the night before, which was Saturday night, one of the main teen leaders from her father's church had gone to sleep on her parents' screened porch. During the night someone cut through the screen, raped and murdered her. It was such a tragedy. Evil forces certainly had launched an all-out attack the last twenty four hours.

It was time for me to take our bus and return the sixty or so miles to Spokane. We had much prayer for safety because that particular highway was extremely dangerous. I left and arrived home with no further incidence.

That fall at the church we were preparing for our annual Halloween party. Having had the experience we had that summer we decided that we would make it a harvest party. Posters were placed in the nearby shopping center announcing the party. On the poster we mentioned it would be a costume party. However, we requested that no costumes related to witches, goblins, ghosts or the occult be worn. We realized that Halloween falls on the eve of All Saints Day and was dedicated to recognizing Satan and the underworld. The desire to eliminate costumes that reflected the underworld, was the reason for the request. The very next day a reporter from the local newspaper came to interview me on the subject. Of course when I read the full page article I realized he had twisted my words making me out to be a crazy Christian fundamentalist. I should have known better than to have given him permission for the interview.

The day of the party arrived. We were really crowded. The costumes were great and no one was turned away Our parties were usually held in the basement all-purpose room. There were swinging doors at the foot of the stairs from the vestibule. A great time was underway when I felt a shiver and strange emotional chill up my spine. Turning toward the doors I noticed a man had entered wearing a black robe with a chain and emblem of a Satanic coven. I approached him. He identified himself as the head warlock of a local coven of Satan worshipers. Interesting, I thought. "I am the high priest of the church of Satan in Spokane," he said. "I have come to tell you that you have publicly maligned our most holy day. I demand an audience with these children to explain that witch craft and its holy arts can be good." I was somewhat taken back, but not totally surprised. I prayed silently, then said to him, "Your father is not God our Father but Satan and I rebuke you in the name of the Lord Jesus Christ Son of God and King of Kings. As a person I would like to share God's love with you, but not in your position as

High Priest of Satan. You can, through Jesus Christ ,be free". Suddenly he began to shudder. He abruptly turned on his heels and ran up the stairs and out the door of the church. I never heard from him again.

DETERMINED TO DIE

The youth group continued to grow. They were attending morning worship, listening for and learning the things of God. However, they were not the usual "church" youth. They did not dress accordingly nor did they possess the requirements of rigid "churchianity." This made the "status quo" ladies very nervous. So set in their "church" ways they let their actions conform not to the Word of God, but to tradition. They lost touch with the compassion of the Lord and the love for souls. This "status quo" attitude controlled their every thought and turned into anger. It all came to a head one Sunday morning.

One of our youth came as usual to the service. She was dressed in a rather short skirt carrying a can of Pepsi in her hand. She went immediately to the front row and sat in the left pew facing the pulpit. There were long center pews with aisles on each side. Smaller pews were next to the windows. There was carpet in the aisles, but the floors were bare. This girl finished her Pepsi before the service began and set it on the floor under her pew. During the service as there was no one else sitting in that small pew, she lay down, listening to the sermon. Meanwhile the clique of "status quo ladies" sat in the back letting their anger steam.

I finished the sermon and during the recessional began walking down the aisle near the girl. As I approached her pew she stopped me and asked me a question. I usually had three major points to support the theme. She asked, "Pastor I understood your first and last point, but am confused about the other. Can you explain it to me?" "Of course. After I greet people we will talk." With that said I proceeded down the aisle to the vestibule at the back to shake hands. Waiting for me were some of the status quo clique who accosted me immediately. "We demand you get rid of that girl and her friends. She is not our kind and we do not want them here." Unfortunately I took the rejection personally and replied in my own fear of rejection. Angrily I ask the spokeslady if she could tell me what the sermon was about. She ignored me and went on with her tirade against the youth. I continued telling her how the girl had listened and was asking spiritual questions. Then I said pointedly, "Who do you think worshipped here this morning? It was that girl, not you. All you ladies did was sit through the service steaming in your prejudice and conniving a way to rid yourselves of these 'sinners'. I think that it is you who should be driven from this church in your self-righteousness, not these precious lost souls who are seeking God." With that said I abruptly turned and left the church for my car. I was shaking and tears were flowing freely down my cheeks Taking matters into their own hands they indicated to the young people that they were not welcome anymore. A summer I thought was a great victory in their lives went down in in the flames of "status quo-we don't do things that way", self-righteousness. Soon all these new youth were gone. I sank lower and lower in depression. The old dungeon of my childhood returned and finally I ended up in a fetal position in the corner of my doctor's office.

CHAPTER FOURTEEN

MINIRTH MEIER PSYCHIATRIC HOSPITAL

APPLYING GRACE AND TRUTH OVER TIME

I did not acknowledge the doctor's entrance. We sat in silence for a few minutes. Finally he asked me what was going on. Slowly, I responded with a minimal of the recent events, the dreams and then for the first time, my past childhood events that had been hidden in my personal dungeon for fifty years. I poured out my story with tears and sobs. I was totally defeated. The breakdown was becoming complete, both mentally and physically. Broken and burnt out I knew of no place to go.

He immediately picked up his office phone and cancelled all other appointments that afternooon. He consulted with my wife and Dr. Helen, our missionary doctor friend. He told me he was not leaving me until I agreed to enter a psychiatric hospital. He, my wife and Dr. Helen, persuaded me that that was the best thing I could do. It was terribly embarrassing, but I realized that I really had no other choice. The next few days were spent in locating a suitable and affordable hospital. We soon learned of Minirth Meier Hospital in North Seattle. The cost was prohibitive. My insurance would cover only the first week of in-patient care. I needed more than three weeks. In consultation with the hospital I was informed of a new program for pastors. They had a large room converted into a small apartment for pastors and their wives. Thus I could use my out-patient insurance. The arrangement was for me to be on a locked ward for one week. Then Marilyn would join me for the next couple weeks or so in the free apartment. After the first week I would spend the nights with Marilyn in our room, go down to the ward by six a.m. and stay until about nine at night. Marilyn would be available for group sessions, couples counseling and didactic seminars. She was also invited to have dinner with me on the ward.

The treatment was wonderful. There was one staff member assigned to each patient. Signing an agreement that I would not attempt suicide nor violate the rules was an absolute requirement. Also I had to agree if things deteriorated enough that they were not able to care for me to be transferred to a State Mental Hospital. Certainly this was the lowest time of my life. All was signed and I arrived in Seattle. My brother and his wife greeted me and transported me to the hospital. Saying good bye to them in the lobby I was escorted onto the locked ward and to my room. It was just in time for dinner. After dinner I met with counselors, my assigned psychiatrist and other staff members.

That first night or two I could not sleep. Walking the hallways was all I could stand. Immediately upon leaving my room a staff member was by my side walking quietly with me, answering questions and listening to my groanings and sobs. He was such a comfort. I had spent most of my childhood and life not being listened to and this was so different. I could not believed that anyone other than my dear wife could care for me like that. After breakfast in the morning there were consultations with doctors, psychiatric tests, and of course didatic. This was the time we were taken into God's Word. From Paul's letters, especially Galatians, Ephesians and Colossians it was poured into us who we really are in Christ,. There were no guilt trips laid upon us. Sin was acknowledged, but we were shown that it was not always our sin. Many times we had been sinned against. The key to my mental health was in truly believing, not just mental knowledge, but truly knowing that we are new creations in Christ. Never before had I grasped the concept of grace without works. Marilyn joined me for these Bible sessions. It was like being in Bible school all over again. Truths I had learned there now were becoming realities.

During other sessions Marilyn was encouraged to tell me how my sin and failure had affected her and how she felt. I had not realized what a terrible burden and hurt all this had been to her. Yes, she was quick to forgive, but that did not remove the pain I had caused over the years.

In addition the patients had role-play sessions. In these we were to contemplate the areas of our own hurt, reveal them and then allow another patient or staff member to play the role of the one we felt had hurt us. We were encouraged to tell them how they had hurt us, scream at them or whatever released the terrible anger each of us had harbored deep within for so many years. Sometimes this was most difficult. There was one lady who had been sexually abused by her pastor. Learning that I was a pastor she transferred all her anger to me. It did not solve her problems. Going deeper into psychois she was transferred to another facility. One person related how she had been forced into Satanic rituals. There was only one other man in the hospital at this time and he was released a couple days later. I then became the only man in the room full of angry women. It was difficult to hear their stories, often with men as the villians. Most were very understanding. At the end of my stay the bond among us was deep and many tears were shed as one by one a friend finished her treatment and was gone usually never to be seen again. I remember them all and they are never far from my thoughts.

Art therapy sessions were revealing as we were required to express our feelings through painting, making door mats, and sculpting clay. I had never realized how cathartic all this was. If there were people in our lives who insisted on controlling us by whatever means possible we were encouraged to confront them. These were difficult phone calls and sometimes, without meaning to, relationships were marred. These were relationships that were not healthy. Some were healed later, some were not.

When the first week was completed and we were allowed to leave the ward, Marilyn, my brother, his wife and our youngest son and his wife took me out to dinner at a nearby restaurant. I was not ready yet. Crying children and the usual noise of a restaurant almost did me in. We had to leave as soon as possible. Walking back to the hospital I had difficulty keeping my balance. However, it was good to see family again.

All was well once we got to our room. I needed to do some confronting which was difficult and brought me to tears. It took many years to rebuild that relationship. It is much better now, but not fully healed. Heaven will be so great as all these things will not be remembered.

Finally my inhouse treatment was completed and I was well enough to return home. Weekly counseling was our choice for many years to come. I was now without work and without income. I tried, but could not get a job. I was still in depression. It was then I applied for social security disability. Many doctors were consulted, both ours and those assigned by Social Security Department. However I was immediately denied. I did not apply again, but hired a lawyer who appealed my case. Another round of doctors' visits and examinations showed that I was deserving of disability payments because I could not hold a job and deserved disability retirement. The doctor recommended, even insisted, that I be approved immediately. Shortly I was called to the Social Security office to see my case worker. In the face of all their own doctors' statements he denied the application saying strangely that he did not like me and that he "owned" my future. I was angry but did not show it. Immediately, however, I phoned my brother in Seattle. He knew someone high up in the state offices of Social Security. Lester had worked as a counseloer for Social Security's office of Indian Affairs for years. The very next day I received a call from the Spokane office telling me that I had been approved and a check for past weeks was in the mail. Further she said that I would no longer be seeing the agent assigned to me as he no longer worked for the Social Security office.

The check did arrive and every month thereafter. These checks have been the main source of income except for the years I returned to part-time ministry.

IN THE PULPIT AGAIN

My dear friend and former pastor, Ed, had been called to be interim pastor of a former liberal church on the south hill. One day he called me and asked me if I would join him as co-pastor. The work was too much for him and the church agreed to bring me on board per his request. We began our work together. I taking much of the week's responsibilities and both of us sharing the pulpit on Sundays. Within a few months Pastor Ed had to move on and I was left with all the pastoral responsibilites.

The concregation had withdrawn from the very liberal United Church of Christ and was for the first time without a denominational affiliation. Through a local pastor friend I learned of the 4 Cs, the Conservative Congregational Christian Church. It had been formed out of the old Congregational Conference back in the '30s in response to the liberal direction their former association was taking. My friend was the Area Pastor for the 4 Cs. I applied for their ministerial credentials which were granted. By the time my pastorate at Lincoln Heights Congregational Church was coming to an end eight years later the church had also joined the 4 Cs and was doing well. It is now Lincoln Heights Community Church.

During our time there we had several youth pastors minister with us. One of them was a young Moody Bible Instute student who came on board. Moody has an extension school here in Spokane. It had formerly been known as the Inland Empire School of the Bible. I had taught missions classes there before it was given over to Moody. Jared was a great young man and walked close with the Lord. Often he would join me in the office while I taught him many of the old hymns. I am sure our secretary was amused as she heard the old favorites sung by two male voices. Our relationship in the Lord became strong. Shortly I met another Moody student, Tiersa, who joined us in ministry to the youth. It so happened that she and Jared had been childhood friends. It was a joy to see their relationship grow. We all encouraged them and after a while he proposed. Jared and Tiersa were married by me in a beautiful farm setting in northern Oregon, near their home town. Tiersa transferred to Biola University, my Alma Mater, and Jared enrolled in Chafer Theological Seminary in Long Beach, Calkifornia. Since I was the local Biola Alumni Chapter Leader I was frequently on campus for meetings. I happened to be present when Tiersa graduated from Biola. They are now serving the Lord in Australia.

One morning I received a phone call at the church from a pastor friend in the area. He informed me that his denomination, Baptist General Conference and North

American Baptist Conference, of which I was still a member, had a joint teaching ministry in Russia bringing Bible School and Seminary Education to various areas of Russia. It was different from how we do things in America. Teachers and staff were sent to different central areas to establish a one year school. Funds raised, mostly by sponsoring churches here in America, were sufficient enough that no tuition was charged. The sponsoring local churches in Russia provided the rooms for the school. There was a great need in Siberia for a teacher and my friend asked me to consider going to Russia the next November. I would be responsible for one semester. Only one subject was taught per semester. However the classes began at 9 a.m. and ended by 9 p.m. every day from Monday through Friday. On weekends the teachers were required to be guest speakers in as many churches as possible. It would be an exhaustive undertaking. After much prayer and promises of financial support by many friends both among the members of Lincoln Heights and other friends I accepted the challenge. This was early in the year so I had plenty of time to prepare. I chose the book of Joshua as the subject for the semester I would teach. In the meantime the daily routine of the church ministry continued.

Before I would leave for Russia, yet unknown to us, we were to face one of our deepest tragedies further learning more of God's grace.

TESTED BY DEATH

One of my best friends had been ill with cancer and was now in his final days at home. His death drew close. When I arrived to be with him early that spring morning I found him conscious. He was saying goodbye to his family. A few hours later he passed away. His family and I sat at their dining room table preparing the details of the funeral. The phone rang. It was Marilyn for me. Her voice was quivering. I asked her what was wrong. "Steve's missing." she answered. Steve, our oldest son, had gone camping on Mica Peak as he frequently did. Steve's problems began late in high school. Being small of stature and a pastor's son, he was often teased by his peers. Adults put unfair expectations upon pastors' kids. Since Steve had a very shy and retiring personallty from early childhood, he was unable to absorb this mistreatment. He turned away from the church kids, who seemed always to hurt him, to non-church friends. One of his church friends was into drinking and drugs. Steve soon learned that his best friends were at the tavern. I am reminded of the theme song of the TV show "Cheers." With comforting words it described the bar as a place where everyone knows your name, where everyone was accepted as they are and everyone was cared for. I often thought that should be the theme of the church, but too often it is not. Churches seem to thrive on cliques, gossip, legalism, and critisim of anyone who does not fit their particular idea of what a Christian should look like and do. This was not true of Steve's drinking buddies. He became an acoholic. Steve had a daughter, Mary, whom he loved dearly. She came into our lives at about three years of age. She soon became the love of Steve's life and they spent many hours together, often camping on Mica Peak. He went into treatment for alcohol addiction at least three times. He and his friends had a club they called The Bozo Club. These were his only friends as his Christian friends had already written him off. So he always returned to the "Bozos" for relationships.

We worried about his drinking and his depression. Everything we could do was done and now out of our control. That's when the phone rang that fateful morning. One of his good friends called Marilyn to tell her that Steve was dead. He had hung himself on Mica Peak at their camp site a couple of nights before. His friends found him when they went looking for him. Though we had been worried about this neither of us were prepared for the reality.

Immediately I related to my friend's family the circumstances surrounding my decision not to hold their husband's and father's funeral. Upon arriving home and comforting Marilyn, sharing many sobs and tears I called our other sons and family with the news. It was a few days before the family gathered at the funeral home to plan the service. As we sat in the director's office, my friend's funeral was underway in the chapel. It seemed like a double blow.

The funeral chapel was packed the day of Steve's service. His former church friends were there. Many confessed to us their regret at how they had treated him. His "Bozo" friends were shattered. The current pastor, John, from Fourth Memorial Church, my childhood and home church along with Pastor Ed, the pastor with whom

I had formerly served at Fourth conducted the funeral. It was beautiful. The gospel was clearly presented. Afterward one of the "Bozos" committed his life to Christ. However, we lost track of him and today do not know if it was real.

Memories of Steve crowded our senses for many days. Steve was an excellent artist. We looked at all his art once again. Much of it was filled with dispair. But there was a special drawing. It was of a cherub baby face in the lower right hand corner staring up at Christ on the cross in the upper left hand corner. I was thrilled with it. I had said to Steve what was my interpretation of it, "It's the Baby Jesus looking into the future." He corrected me, "No, Dad, that's me. I am the babe who believed in Him, but I have never .grown.." Without saying a word I just hugged him that day.

Now fresh from standing over Steve's grave I berated myself for having not been the father I should have been. No chance now to redeem myself.

Now what? For the moment going to Russia was the last thing I wanted to do. However, I did not rush to a decision. There was still the church to which I must minister. Our three remaining sons and their families needed comfort. Marilyn needed me. Did everyone need me? Was I up to the task? I could only rely on the grace of the Lord.

Sermons were to be prepared, youth ministry went on under another youth leader, Bible classes had to be taught and the routine must go on. Slowly the pain resided. The day by day dwelling on our loss, our disappointment and our anger subsided. Things returned to what was perceived to be normal. With Marilyn's encouragement and that of my friends I decided to go ahead with the Russian ministry.

RUSSIA

My passport was obtained, visas secured, tickets were purchased, bags packed, Joshua notes in hand and goodbyes said. Marilyn saw me off at the Spokane International Airport. A short layover in Seattle and a few hours flight found me in New York City's International Airport. The plane was full of Russians and a few others. One couple was headed to Moscow to pick up their adopted child. Their excitement was contagious. I found my seat on the Delta flight from New York to Moscow, Russia. Already tired from the first and second legs of the trip I was looking forward to some sleep over the fifteen hours' flight. And sleep I did except for some very good meals. By the time we landed in Moscow a full day had passed and it was early evening on a Friday.

After passing customs I was met at the airport by a man yelling my name which he had printed on a sign he was holding. He had his car out front. Quickly we entered the feverish traffic as it was rush hour. Speeding past Red Square we drove for some time before entering the compound of the Russian Baptist Seminary. It was dinner time. After a very good meal which was strange to me, I was introduced to Dmitri, who was to be my guide for Saturday's tour of Moscow and after I returned from Siberia to Moscow. My room was a regular seminary room with a common bath and shower down the hall.

After breakfast the next morning the students left for their student assignments. Dmitri, a teacher returning from his semester of teaching and I headed into Moscow to see the sights. It was early December. An unusual cold front had descended upon Moscow and most of Russia. We arrived at Red Square. It is a wide square with a beautiful Russian Orthodox Cathedral, statues and government buildings. Underneath the square is a very modern and large shopping mall. At the gate stood several very well uniformed Russian solders who escorted us in. Dmitri related to me how they had not been paid for six months, yet were faithful every day to carry out their duties.

Behind one of the buildings on the Square was the Russian tribute to her fallen soldiers including their first cosmonaut.

Waiting for admission we stood before the majestic cathedral. Upon entering I was amazed at how marvelous it is. It reminded me of the Russian Orthodox Church in Bethelem, Israel, that I had visited some years before, ornate and cold inside.

It was time for some food. We walked out of the Square and up a busy street. Finding a Pizza Hut we ordered several pizzas. There was so much left over we took the rest back to the seminary students. Along the way Dmitri told me of his home town, Archangel on the coast. In his teens he was instrumental in building a church there. Now he was preparing for the ministry. I bought a few souvenirs that day as I was headed to Siberia. I left money with Dmitri and he promised to purchase some nesting dolls, called Matryoshka dolls. They are all hand painted and fit inside one another. These among a few other souvenirs he would have for me when I returned from Siberia.

Early the next morning I boarded a brand new Russian airline 737 Boeing jet liner for Omck, the largest city in Siberia. It was the most luxurious flight I have ever taken. Being new everything was immaculate. The meals were superb with Filet Mignon steak for dinner. As we neared Omck, pronounced Omsk, the pilot informed us that the air temperature outside was 70 degrees below zero Fahrenheit. When the door was opened we felt the blast of extremely cold wind. Carefully stepping down the stairs we entered a non-heated bus for the ride to the terminal. Someone was there to get me and take me to my host's apartment. The elevator did not work so we climbed eight or nine flights of stairs. He said that a car would come for me by eight in the morning. My host had prepared for me a simple but nutritious meal so early in the morning. I was shown my room and retired under heavy quilts, just like I had as a boy. After breakfast which included delicious black bread my car arrived. It was so bitterly cold that I had every piece of skin covered. It took only a few minutes for the car's heater to warm up. Snow and ice covered the ground. A short time later we arrived at the First Baptist Church of Omck. It was large with several stories. We were so far north that the sun arose on the horizon around 10 a.m. and set about 2 p.m. The classroom had no windows so at each five minute break everyone gathered at the hall window to drink in the sun light.

I had a new interpreter, a young nineteen-year-old lad. He was already married and had full command of English including American idioms. I provided him with a written text of my lessons on Joshua which he studied every night. When interpreting he rarely missed an idiom. It was such a pleasure. When using an interpreter in Japan I had to be careful not to use idioms. Sasha however knew most all of them. I was very impressed when he told me he had never left Russia. He also spoke English without an accent. Sometime later both Sasha and Dmitri came to America to study for the ministry.

Getting to know the class I discovered that of the twenty nine students, mostly men, fifteen had been in prison. Of the fifteen ex-prisoners all but one returned to the prison everyday to conduct Bible studies and worship services. It appears that when the communists imprisoned evangelical pastors, those pastors preached the gospel and set up prison churches winniing many young men to the Lord. Some of these men were now my students. There was one, however, who was not teaching Bible in the prison. He stated that after Bible School here he needed to return to the town in which he committed the crime. There he would live for a year demonstrating by his life what Christ can do to redeem a man. Then he would return to prison to serve the prison church there.

Lunch and dinner at the school were delicious. I loved the thick vegetable soup served and the bread was out of this world. I learned, however, not to eat too much at the school. When I returned to my host later that first evening she also had dinner prepared. One morning she had hard boiled eggs. Eggs were hard to come by and expensive. She had purchased one for herself and Anna as well so that I would not feel embarrassed. Good friends were made there with whom I still have contact.

On weekends I was ferried to various churches to preach. One Saturday evening we went to a church in

Omck. It was a large church yet had little if any heat and the bath room was a large outhouse in the back. At 70 degrees below zero it was an interesting task to use them. The typical Russian church service is two hours long with three sermons, much singing by numerous choirs and tender poems recited by the ladies. The congregation had on fur coats and ushenkas, Russian fur hats. However, tradition dictated that pastors wear only black suits. My church had provided me with warm long-johns but they were not sufficient for the deep cold. Also my head was bare which added to my discomfort. On one Sunday we drove into the country to a farm village. I was required to surrender my passport to the Omck police while in Siberia. Thus I was concerned as we approached a check point manned by soldiers with rifles and machine guns. As told I sat in the back seat with my ushenka pulled down low and waited. The guard asked the driver for papers, but did not ask the rest of us. When we returned the post was not manned. Leaving the check point we soon entered a birch forest. These glorious white and black trees were set in deep snow. The forest was unbelievably beautiful.

Our first stop was the Baptist church in small farm village. There were three entrance rooms to keep the cold out. Inside a warm wood stove made it very cozy. As before, the service was two hours long. During my sermon an older lady stood up and announced that she needed to repent. She came to the front and knelt while the local pastor counseled her. Then the service resumed. Born again believers in Russia are often called "the repenters". After the service we were served lunch and sent on our way.

Our next stop was a house church in an apartment area. It was crowded with people in a warm, close, and friendly atmosphere. Another two hours, some good food and we returned to Omck.

As the days went on I was becoming quite sick. My sinuses were inflamed, my chest was tight and my throat raw. We sought out a drug store and bought some medicine, but it did not help. By the final day, after exam results were given I could not continue. Going back to my host's apartment I went right to bed. Kapitolina and Anna cared for me as best they could. Anna's father, a dentist out of work came also. I had brought several men's suits as requested to give to needy pastors. Anna's father had been out of work for some time. The government social medicine program had failed so dentists, and doctors were out of work. Preparing for my return to Moscow I counted the money I still had. There was plenty. I took the rest and gave it to Kapotolina's son, the dentist. It turned out to be more than he would make in two months on Russia's socialist salary.

Early the next Saturday morning I boarded the plane for my trip back to Moscow. I was getting weaker by the hour. Arriving back at the seminary I was given a very small room in a run-down hotel next door. Dmitri brought me the things I had asked him to buy and asked if I wanted to go into the city again. Seeing how sick I was we decided not to go, but to say our goodbyes there.

This small room had a single bed on one wall, a table just a foot away on the other wall, a very small electric heater and a hot plate. Thinking that I may be responsible for some of my meals Marilyn had prepared some "glorified oatmeal" for me with raisons, nuts and powdered milk mixed in. However, after I poured some hot water from the kettle into a bowl of that stuff, I could not eat it. So sick was I that I left a note on the table with instructions for what to do with my body should I die in the night.

I did not die, but boarded the Delta flight the next day and headed home. There were very few on the plane to New York so I took a seat away from the others. Another American passenger was also coughing and wheezing so he joined me. The other passengers kept us supplied with cough drops all the way to New York.

Interestingly enough, I do not remember anything between New York and my arrival in Spokane. Immediately Marilyn took me to the doctor. He was going to put me in the hospital, but instead loaded me up with antibiotics and ordered me to bed with instructions to stay there. That I willingly did. When I was well enough I was summoned to the Health District office and underwent tests for tuberculosis, which were positive. Six months of daily and then semi weekly shots of antibiotics were required before I was declared cured.

It had only been a few months since Steve's death. I continued at Lincoln Heights Church. My youth director, Jared and his new wife Teresa had moved to California. It was my privilege to visit them when I was there for a board meeting at the University. I continued for some time as Alumni Chapter Leader for BIOLA, attempting to gather alumni together from the Inland Empire area in eastern Washington and northern Idaho. I was getting more tired as I grew older so finally I had to drop that work. I still represent Biola University at the local Christian College Fair in Spokane each year.

Finally I resigned from Lincoln Heights after eight years as pastor. I needed to retire. However that did not last long as I was called to be interim pastor of a Baptist church in Couer d' Alene, Idaho. Two years later we secured a new pastor from Biola's Talbot Theological Seminary. After he was installed I retired again. This time for good.

CHAPTER FIFTEEN

FINAL MEMORIES

ISRAEL

The Holy Land. I had dreamt of seeing Jerusalem, Galilee, the Jordan river and all of Israel. The chance to go came in the 1980's when one of my church members asked if I wanted to go on a pastors' orientation trip to Israel. The only requirement for this all expense paid adventure was that I gather and lead a tour there in the near future. Of course I jumped at it. I took my two weeks vacation early and signed up.

There were thirty of us pastors and Christian workers in the group. Several from Spokane rode with me to Seattle. There we boarded a 747 Boing jet for the first leg of the journey. This was a non-stop flight to Copenhagen. A two-hour layover and we took off for Ben Gurion International in Tel Aviv, Israel. We landed in early evening.

Boarding a tour bus we drove up the mountain to Jerusalem which is at 2500 feet above sea level. Even though we were tired our tour director took us up mount Scopos. From a lovely view point we looked down upon the Holy City, Old Jerusalem. The walls were all lit in brilliant flood lights. The Wailing Wall was just below us with the steps going up to the Temple Mount. Silence surrounded our group. We were speechless. There was a real sense of God's presence which brought tears to our eyes.

From there we were taken to our hotel near the old city. Dinner was served and we retired to our rooms. I was suddenly and rudely awakened at about four or a.m. by the wailing sound of the call to morning prayers from the Muslim Mineret just outside my window. The next morning I slept through it. Breakfast consisted of goat cheese, hard boiled eggs, delicious bread, jam and coffee.

By eight a.m. we boarded our tour bus and headed down to the Jordan Valley and the Dead Sea 2000 feet below sea level. Half way down our bus stopped at a turn off. An Arab Bedoin was standing there with his trusty camel on a rope. For one dollar each we could mount the camel, ride in circles for a bit and dismount. Of course the appropriate pictures were taken. I am hyper-active so I did not wait for the camel to kneel completely before I jumped off. The camel owner screamed at me and the camel spit in my face. Ugh! I had much to learn about riding a camel.

We continued down to the valley and followed along the Dead Sea to Masada. This was where the Jews made their final stand against Rome in AD 70. King Herod had a palace on the thousand foot high mesa. Determined not to surrender they held out for three years before the Romans built ramps and succeeded climbing over the walls. However, it was a hallow victory as all had committed suicide rather than surrender to Rome. Because of their bravery Israel commissions its military officers and men on top of Masada every year.

There are two ways up Masada. One is a narrow path and the other a cable car. Since I am afraid of heights I chose the cable car which hung 1000 feet above the desert floor at one point. I chose the pole in the middle, wrapped my hands securely around it and did not look out the windows. The cable car ended on Masada, about fifteen feet below the rim. We had to climb a narrow path to the top. I hugged the rock side and refused to look down. The mesa was huge. There were many grain storage ruins, cisterns for water and colorful tiled baths. At the north end was King Herod's palace. It was elaborate in its day with steam baths tiled and painted murals on the walls. Standing near the edge, but not too close, I watched a flight of Israeli fighter jets as they flew low overhead with a great roar. They were heading for Lebanon to the fighting. Israel was just concluding there. Next to me was a tall military officer with a large hand radio to his ear. He told me he was a ground coordinator for the jets that had just headed north. The war was about over and Israel was withdrawing her troops back to Jerusalem.

We rode the cable car back down to the parking lot and again boarded our bus. A short drive up the coast of the Dead Sea is Engedi. This is where King Saul was sleeping in a cave when David found him and cut off the hem of his robe. David could have killed him but he did not want to touch "God's anointed" king. At Engedi was a rocky beach and dressing area for swimmers. I tried to swim which was quite easy as I could not lower much of my body into the very salty water. I just floated. It was a weird sensation. I showered off in the open showers afterward, but could not get rid of the salt on my body. It took several days in my hotel shower to finally get rid of it.

The next day we returned to the Jordan River to visit Galilee. At Nazareth we shopped at a souvenir shop across the street from the First Church of the Nazarene. Jacob's Well had been escavated and was fifteen feet below current ground level. The home of Mary's parents had been unearthed as well. From there we went to Tiberius and took a boat across the Sea of Galilee to Capernaum which was the Apostle Peter's home. We anchored in the middle of the lake where Peter and his family often fished.

Suddenly the famous Galilean wind arose and tossed our ferry around.

At Capernaum we found an excavated tile flooring of an ancient church. It displayed the feeding of the five thousand. Climbing a small hill was a Church commemorating the Sermon on the Mount. I managed to slip away into a small grove of trees where Jesus had preached that message. Sitting on a stone bench alone with a gentle breeze from off the Sea of Galilee I was nearly transported in my imagination to that very day. It was so peaceful and the air seemed itself to be holy.

On our way back to Jerusalem we had lunch in a Kibbutz. By the way, the Jordan Valley was full of rose farms reminding me of the prophecy that the desert would blossom like a rose. Further on we visited an often frequented place on the shore of the Jordan where a baptism was underway. Tourists and others gathered here to be baptized in the Jordan River. It was not the site of Jesus' baptism as that is in the territory of the country of Jordan.

About mid-day we arrived at Jericho for lunch. From there the tour was to go on to view the walls of Jericho and other sights in the area. However, for me it was not to be. Suddenly as we were eating lunch a shout came from the restroom area. I was called as I at that time was a First Responder with a rural fire department back home. Our American tour guide had collapsed. The Arab tour guide was much disturbed as we could not revive him. An ambulance was called and I volunteered to leave the tour and accompany him to the hospital in Jerusalem, which was at the top of the steep and curvy highway from the Dead Sea to Jerusalem. The local emergency room walls in Jericho were bullet pocked from previous battles. The ambulance was no more than a panel truck with the stretcher in back. Next to the stretcher an Arab held in place both the stretcher and a large oxygen bottle loosely tied to the back of the front seat. I sat in the passenger's seat. There were no seat belts. Our Arab driver drove furiously up the mountain at full speed. The siren was not automatic so he had to use one hand to push the button. Since Israel was pulling out of Lebanon the narrow highway was full of very slow moving flatbed trucks carrying huge armored tanks. Our driver did not slow down, but pushed the siren button and swerved into on coming traffic around the tanks. Cars, mules, camels, people and geese fled to the side as we rushed past. My hands were white as I gripped the handle in front of me. Taking a shortcut through small villages we suddenly came out onto a wide Jerusalem street and squealed right. Not soon enough for me we arrived at the hospital. Our patient was admitted, still mostly "out-of-it".

The Arab tour leader explained that there was no way I could return to the day's tour but I was welcome to come to his home to wait the several hours before their return. At the time I did not know that visiting in an Arab home was breaking the law. I readily accepted. His home was lovely, well furnished and big. The food was plenteous and delicious. Before returning to my hotel that evening he warned me not to answer any questions at the the airport departure about being in an Arab home. The visit was enlightening, to say the least, as I learned the Palestinian side of the story.

By now it was Sunday and we attended Christian worship service at a Jerusalem church. That afternoon we went to Bethlehem. There were two cathedrals, one Greek Orthodox and the other Russian Orthodox side by side. These two churches have been fighting over who owns the cave in which Jesus was born. A stone wall divides the cave. On one side is the cave of St. Jerome and the other the Manger. The actual manger was not a wooden feeding box, but an oblong hole hewn into the rock of the cave. To feed the animals' hay was placed in it. This was where Jesus was born among the stalls of animals.

Many souvenir stores lined the town square. I purchased some black ear rings for Marilyn made from black stones found only in the area of Bethlehem. We visited a cave where shepherds held their sheep. There were many in the area. Exhausted from the weeks whirlwind tour I eagerly went to sleep. The next day we were visited the Old City. The streets were very narrow and filled with people, carts and donkeys laden with wares. All the traditional sights brought the Word of God into realistic focus. The Hall of Flagelation where Pilate had Jesus scurged, the Pool of Siloam, various churches and holy places spoke of the Lord's presence. Finally we ventured outside of the Old City, seeing the upper room, the Garden of Gethsemane, the home of the High Priest and the Garden Tomb. Sitting in a gathering spot we could see Golgotha to the right and the empty tomb to the left. Some of our group were singers and began to sing. We were served communion in wooden cups which we all took home.

About ten days after we had departed Seattle our tour prepared to leave Israel. Getting up at four a.m. we arrived at the airport in Tel Aviv around six. Two lines were formed to go through the check points. As I drew closer I could hear the questions asked those in front of me. The dreaded one about being in an Arab home was read to everyone from a hand held clip-board the armed guard carried. I mouthed a silent prayer. Asking the Lord what to do. I did not need an answer because the Lord took care of it Himself.

I stood in front of the guard answering all her questions. To my surprised delight she did not ask me the dreaded question. I had decided to tell the truth which would have meant my being detained perhaps for several days to be questioned about all that was said in the tour guide's home. Realizing the intervention of the Lord I could have flown home without wings.

COPENHAGEN

Our layover in Denmark this time was more than twenty four hours. We had plenty of time to see the local sights and do some shopping. The first place I wanted to see was the statue of Hans Christian Anderson in downtown Copenhagen. Years later a very sweet man in my congregation related that he was born in Copenhagen and as a boy sat on the lap of the statue. I told him that I had done the same and had a picture of it. I gave that picture to him as he was drawn back to his childhood.

There were the palace, the famous Tivoli theme park, amazing cathedrels and many other sights to see in one day. Our hotel was only a block from the very famous walking street in downtown Copenhagen. It is paved with cobblestone and no cars, except little three wheelers are allowed. Of course it is a tourist "trap" but I didn't mind. Shops of all kinds, theaters, smoke shops and clothing stores begged for our attention. I looked everywhere for a special gift for Marilyn but nothing caught my fancy. So I returned to my hotel room empty handed.

After dinner that evening I wandered through the lobby and into the gift shop. In one of the display cases was the perfect gift. It was a necklace, bracelet and ear ring set made of hand painted porcelain. The design was blue figures on white. Blue is Marilyn's favorite color. Even though it was expensive I could not resist and bought it for her.

The next day we flew directly to Seattle. I picked up my car and passengers and drove the three hundred miles to Spokane. It took a week to unwind. I took numerous slides as well as purchasing a slide program about Israel which I arranged into a slide-show report of the trip. This was one of the high lights of my life.

EPILOGUE

WRAPPING UP THE THEME

GRACE OVER THE LONG RUN

Understanding God's grace is not easy. We are prone to insert personal works into the equation. However to do so is to dilute grace. God's grace is complete. Either salvation is absolutely His doing and His only or it is not grace. Paul is clear that it is by grace that we are saved not by works. Yet we qualify grace by our works. Agreeing that we can do nothing to earn God's grace we accept His grace in the sacrifice of His Son, Jesus Christ, and His death and Resurrection as ours. But somehow we revert to works for the rest of our lives. We qualify grace with the idea we have to *do* something to maintain our salvation and deserve eternal life. That is far from the truth. Even arbitrary things as a certain kind of worship, or a conscribed dress, or some sort of approved activity are substituted for a life of grace. If someone does not conform to our way of thinking then we become critical of them, thus making our own works to shine. Many have used the term. "accepting Christ as our personal Savior." The issue is *believing*. "Whosoever *believes* in Me," Jesus said, "has eternal life." We not only believe in His substitution death on the cross and His resurrection, but we must believe and rest completely in His eternal grace.

There will always be failures along the way. Failures are sin. It is God's unconditional Grace that brings us back every time. We must recognize that we are not our own, but His. Living for Him is not a drudgery of works, but a joyous obedience. We know that we will never be holy enough to deserve salvation. We depend totally on His love and grace. He has declared that no one who comes to Him shall ever be cast out. Should we walk away from Him for a time it is His grace that will always draw us back.

His grace is absolutely Grace Over the Long Run, never the short. Though we do not know the future, not even of our own actions, the Lord does. He knows our failures and sins, past, present and future. That is why there are no qualifications for salvation. Believing in His constant grace and forgiveness is sufficient. To believe that every big or little sin will remove us from His grace is foolish. Our salvation depends completely on God and Him alone, not on any works of ours either to attain salvation or to maintain it. Anything less than that detracts from His grace. Why are so many Christians depressed, ritualistic and angry? Simply because one has some standard of behavior, it does not bring us eternal salvation. Such behavior only serves to measure oneself and criticize those who do not live up to our rules. Living for Christ is not an obligation but a privilege derived from understanding His grace in all it's fullness. The answer to the first question of the Westminster Shorter Catechism is that man's chief end is to glorify God and enjoy Him forever. Full grace allows us to do that.

What does the future hold for us? No one knows, only God. And if He knows the beginning from the end will He not complete the work he has begun in each one who believes in Him? Marilyn and I celebrated our fiftieth wedding anniversary three years ago. All the kids and the nine grandchildren were there as well as many friends. Seventeen Pontius' crowded into the little church that Sunday. How many years we have left neither of us know. The physical body gets weaker, pain becomes the norm and old age creeps on. Underneath are the Everlasting Arms. Grace Over the Long Run? Yes!